The Cornell Manual for Lifeboatmen, Able Seamen, and Qualified Members of Engine Department

D0905883

The CORNELL MANUAL
for Lifeboatmen, Able Seamen, and Qualified Members of Engine Department

Second Edition

JOHN M. KEEVER

Based on the first edition by
William B. Hayler, John M. Keever,
and Paul M. Seiler

CORNELL MARITIME PRESS
Centreville, Maryland

Library of Congress Cataloging-in-Publication Data

Keever, John M.
    The Cornell manual for lifeboatmen, able seamen, and qualified
members of engine department / John M. Keever.— 2nd ed.
        p. cm.
    Rev. ed. of: Cornell manual for lifeboatmen, able seamen, and
qualified members of engine department / William B. Hayler. 1st
ed. 1984.
    Includes bibliographical references.
    ISBN 978-0-87033-559-4
    1. Lifesaving—Handbooks, manuals, etc. 2. Lifeboat crew
members—Handbooks, manuals, etc. 3. Seamanship—Handbooks,
manuals, etc. 4. Marine engines—Handbooks, manuals, etc. I.
Hayler, William B., 1921– Cornell manual for lifeboatmen, able
seamen, and qualified members of engine department. II. Title.
    VK1445.K44 2004
    363.12'381—dc22
                                                        2004016524

Manufactured in the United States of America
First edition, 1984. Second edition, 2004;
Second printing, 2007

Contents

Foreword

For many years the *Manual for Lifeboatmen, Able Seamen, and Qualified Members of Engine Department, CG-175*, was published by the Coast Guard and was *the* authoritative study guide for the ordinary seaman who was studying for his lifeboatman's or able seaman's examination. It was in handy hip-pocket form and was the seaman's constant companion. Last published in 1972 and little changed since the 1965 edition, it is now out of print and unobtainable.

The authors, in conjunction with Cornell Maritime Press, have succeeded in creating a modern version of this useful booklet and have produced a manual that the seaman can still carry with him. In doing so they have retained portions of the old CG-175, which are still pertinent and have brought it up-to-date by drawing freely on the *American Merchant Seaman's Manual*, the Maritime Administration's *Marine Fire Prevention, Firefighting and Fire Safety*, other public documents, and their own seagoing and teaching background.

Everyone aboard ship should know the elements of seamanship and be prepared to take his place in the lifeboat crew, in the emergency squad, or in firefighting. In order to be qualified to be a part of the crew of any American-flag vessel, a man or woman must obtain an endorsement on a Mariner's Document as lifeboatman or able seaman.

A thorough familiarity with the contents of this manual will provide for the merchant seaman not only the means to obtain the desired endorsements, but also a valuable base on which to build further reading and experience. Of perhaps even greater value will be the encouragement, in the process, of practices of safety at sea.

George W. Jahn
Rear Admiral, U.S. Maritime Service
Master, S.S. *Jeremiah O'Brien*
1944 Normandy 1994

Acknowledgments

Updating the old *Lifeboatman's Manual* (CG-175) and keeping the *Cornell Manual* current has required the assistance of many individuals and organizations in the San Francisco Bay area and elsewhere in the country. If the maritime community were not the closely knit and loyal organization that it is, the task would have been far more difficult. In particular I acknowledge my debt to my colleagues at the California Maritime Academy: Louis C. Jacobi, who wrote the "First Aid" section; Marty Gipson and Midshipman Gini Gatejene, who have drawn many of the sketches that accompany the text; and Midshipman Brian Goldman for his photographs. Additionally, I thank Captain Sam Shaw, Captain Dave Sears, Captain Bob Stewart, Professor Brian Law, and Harriet Millett for lending a hand.

Of the many individuals and firms who have lent their assistance, I particularly wish to thank Charles Regal, Matson Navigation Company, William F. Schill, Chevron Shipping Company; William Martin, RFD Elliot Inc; Bruce Seaton, Defense Mapping Agency; Victoria Darnell, John Sabella & Associates, Inc.; Dean Cooper, Akron Brass Co.; Captain Joseph Murphy, Massachusetts Maritime Academy; and LCDR Robert E. Davila, USCG, Marine Safety Office, San Francisco Bay.

The Cornell Manual for Lifeboatmen, Able Seamen, and Qualified Members of Engine Department

1. Lifeboatman

Disaster may strike suddenly and take many forms. Fires, collisions, explosions, and sinkings are not announced ahead of time, but they take their toll in death and injuries. For this reason, every American ship has a station bill giving the alarm signals and setting forth the emergency duties for each member of the crew.

Station Bills and Muster Lists

When you join a ship, learn your job immediately, and in the event of emergency, know your responsibilities as set forth in the station bill. You must also know the alarm signals. (A numbered card should be fixed on each berth or issued to each crew member at the time of reporting aboard so that you will know your individual duties in case of danger.)

The lifeboatman in charge of each lifeboat or life raft must have a muster list giving the name and abandon ship duties of each member of his lifeboat crew. These duties, set forth in the station bill and muster list, include assembling and guiding the passengers and assisting them with the adjustment of their life preservers. The usual procedure is to have the muster list for each boat typed and then laminated or placed in plastic to protect it from the weather.

A sample station bill giving the standard emergency signals and examples of how duties should be assigned follows (fig. 1). The master may prescribe other signals in the station bill that he or she deems necessary, such as signals for assembling the emergency squad. The individual duties would

MATSON NAVIGATION COMPANY

STATION BILL

S.S. ___[MU]___

FORM NO. V-20-2
PRINTED IN U.S.A.

2489730

SIGNALS

FIRE OR EMERGENCY—Continuous Sounding of Ship's Whistle and Continuous Ringing of GENERAL ALARM Bell for at least 10 Seconds, Preceded and/or Followed by Location Signal:

1 Short Ring on General Alarm Bell	. . . . .	FIRE FORWARD
2 Short Rings on General Alarm Bell	. . . . .	FIRE AMIDSHIPS
3 Short Rings on General Alarm Bell	. . . . .	FIRE AFT
4 Short Rings on General Alarm Bell		

ABANDON SHIP—7 Short Blasts followed by 1 Long Blast on Ship's Whistle accompanied by the Same Signal on the General Alarm Bell
MAN OVERBOARD—5 Short Blasts on Ship's Whistle and 5 Short Rings on General Alarm Bell
DISMISS FROM ANY DRILL—3 Short Blasts on Ship's Whistle and 3 Short Rings on General Alarm Bell

LOWER BOATS . . .	.	1 Short Whistle Blast
STOP LOWERING BOATS	.	2 Short Whistle Blasts

INSTRUCTIONS

1. Immediately upon Reporting Aboard for Duty Ascertain Your Emergency Stations and Duties. Become Familiar with the Layout of the Vessel and the Quickest Means of Proceeding to Your Station from Your Normal Place of Work or Quarters.
2. All Drills on this Vessel Will Simulate Actual Emergency Conditions. Order Must be Maintained at All Drills.
3. Upon Hearing Emergency Signal Proceed Quickly and Safely to Your Emergency Station.
4. EMERGENCY SQUAD Assemble with Designated Equipment at Scene of Fire under Direction of Chief Officer. Emergency Equipment on this Vessel is Stowed SECOND DECK, OUTSIDE CO-2 ROOM.
5. Men Manning Deck Fire Stations, not in Fire Area, Stand By Hydrant and Await Orders of Officer in Charge.
6. Men on Watch Remain on Watch Until Relieved.
7. IN CASE OF FIRE—Sound Alarm at Once—Stop All Blowers—Close All Kingpost Dampers and Trim All Cowl Ventilators Off the Wind—Start Fire Pumps—Close All Airports and Weather Doors—ISOLATE—EXTINGUISH—COOL.
8. FOR MAN OVERBOARD—Hail and Pass the Word "MAN OVERBOARD" to the Bridge. Throw Illuminated Ring Buoys Over, Post Lookout Aloft, Stop Engines (if conditions warrant.) Deck Department and Emergency Squad Muster at Lee Lifeboat.
9. Wear Your Lifejacket to All Abandon Ship Drills, Lifejacket Must Be Worn, or Carried, to All Other Drills.
10. Crew Members are Interdependent, one upon the other, in Any Emergency. Learn to Perform Your Emergency Duties in a Competent Manner. Familiarity with the Proper Use of Emergency Equipment May Save a Life. It Could Be YOURS! All Crew Members will Assist as Required by the Officer in Charge Until the Signal for Dismissal is Sounded.
11. Steward's Department to Arouse, Warn and Direct Passengers to Lifeboat Stations—Seeing They are Warmly Dressed and Lifejackets Properly Adjusted.

DECK DEPARTMENT

RATING	CARD No.	FIRE AND EMERGENCY DUTIES	CARD/BOAT No.	BOAT No.	ABANDON SHIP DUTIES
	-A-	IN COMMAND		-A-	IN COMMAND
MASTER	1	MUSTER EMERGENCY SQUAD, IN CHARGE AT SCENE OF FIRE.	1	2	IN COMMAND, IN CHARGE LOWERING ALL BOATS.
CHIEF OFFICER	1	IN CHARGE FORWARD DECK, BOW TO AFT END ROW #1, FRAME 155.	1	1	IN COMMAND. IN CHARGE AT SCENE OF FIRE.
SECOND OFFICER	2	IN CHARGE FORWARD DECK, BOW TO AFT END ROW #1, FRAME 155.	2	1	SECOND IN COMMAND, MUSTER CREW, CLEAR & LOWER BOAT.

ABLE SEAMAN	20			"K DECK TO SECURE GRIPE.
ABLE SEAMAN	21			"K TO SECURE GRIPE.
...				"TO GRIPE.

ENGINE DEPARTMENT

			20		
			21		

CHIEF ENGINEER	101	IN CHARGE OF ENGINE ROOM.	101	1	IN CHARGE PROPELLING MACHINERY.
FIRST ASSISTANT	102	IN CHARGE CONTROLS, CO-2 SMOTHERING SYSTEM.	102	2	STOP ALL PUMPS WITH OVERBOARD DISCHARGE ABOVE WATERLINE.
SECOND ASSISTANT	103	FORWARD MACHINERY ROOM — IN CHARGE FIRE PUMPS.	103	1	OPERATE MOTOR IN LIFEBOAT
THIRD ASSISTANT	104	ENGINE ROOM — IN CHARGE FIRE PUMPS ...RGER	11..		"G LIFERAFT—IN CHARGE LAUNCHING AFTER LIFERAFT #2.
THIRD ASSISTANT	105	ENGINE ROOM — ASSIST CHIEF "F"	116		"PT—ASSIST WITH LAUNCHING AFTER LIFERAFT #2.
THIRD ASSISTANT	106	ENGINE ROOM — ASSIST ("	117		"IST WITH LAUNCHING AFTER LIFERAFT #2.
CHIEF ELECTRICIAN	107	EMERGENCY GENERA""	118		
SECOND ELECTRICIAN	108	EMERGENCY S""	119		"P FAST AFTER FRAPPING LINE.
REEFER MAINTENANCE	109	REEFER '	120		" AFTER FRAPPING LINE.
UNLICENSED JR. ENGINEER	110	E0""	121		"STERN, ATTEND CRANK WHEN HOISTING.
UNLICENSED JR. ENGINEER	111'		122		"., ATTEND CRANK WHEN HOISTING.
UNLICENSED JR. ENGINE"					"D CRANK WHEN HOISTING.
WIPER					

STEWARD'S DEPARTMENT

WIPER"				
CHIEF STEWARD	201	CLOSE WEATHER DOORS AFTER HOUSE, STANDBY HOSPITAL	201	1	LEAD OUT SEA PAINTER AS FAR AS POSSIBLE.
CHIEF COOK	202	SECURE GALLEY RANGES, ATTEND STRETCHER"	...		"OAD OUT SEA PAINTER AS FAR AS POSSIBLE.
SECOND COOK & BAKER	203	CLOSE WATERTIGHT DOORS, 2ND D*"	209		"PAINTER FROM BOAT DECK, ATTEND CRANK WHEN HOISTING.
ASSISTANT COOK/MESSMAN	204	CLOSE WATERTIGHT DOORS, '	210		"P FROM BOAT DECK, ATTEND CRANK WHEN HOISTING.
SALOON WAITER	205	FIRE HYDRANTS #19 '	211		"ODER, ATTEND CRANK WHEN HOISTING, PROVIDE BLANKETS.
CREW MESSMAN	206	FIRE HYDRANTS ...TION OF FIRE STATIONS	212		ATTEND CRANK WHEN HOISTING, PROVIDE BLANKETS.
OFFICERS B.R.	207	CLOSE WEA" ...ASTLE HEAD, ABREAST ANCHOR WINDLASS			"D CRANK WHEN HOISTING, PROVIDE BLANKETS.
STEWARD UTILITY	208	FIRE ' — UPPER DECK, ON HATCH COAMING, ROW #3	301		"NK WHEN HOISTING, PROVIDE BLANKETS.
	209	' — UPPER DECK, PORT SIDE, ON HATCH COAMING ROW #12	302		
		#20 — UPPER DECK, STBD SIDE, ON HATCH COAMING ROW #14	303		
	.503	#37 — UPPER DECK, STERN, NEAR STORES HATCH			
		#53 & #54 — UPPER DECK, ABREAST GANGWAY.			

NOTES: 1. Any rating not carried on a vessel is to be marked "Not Carried" or stricken out.
2. Additional ratings are to be inserted in appropriate blank spaces provided for the purpose.
3. For additional information see NOTICE entitled STATION BILLS AND REPORTS OF MASTERS, FORM CG 809A (or B)

MASTER

Fig. 1. The station bill for S.S. *Maui*, 26,665-deadweight-ton containership owned by Matson Navigation Company. Courtesy Matson Navigation Company.

be those considered appropriate by each shipmaster to meet the needs of the vessel.

STCW (Standards of Training, Certification, and Watchkeeping for Seafarers)

International regulatory changes have taken place that impact many of the requirements for certification of lifeboatmen, able seamen, and qualified members of the engine department (QMEDs). The new international system was initiated by the International Maritime Organization (IMO) in 1995 and adopted by the United States in 1998. From 1998 until 2002, a transition took place, and now the new rules apply to everyone. You will see reference to STCW in the requirement sections of this manual, and appendix A contains extracts from the SCTW code. In most cases the rules apply to any certificate for seamen serving aboard a vessel that will operate in foreign ports or outside the U.S. territorial waters.

Lifeboatman Certification and Requirements

Certification required. Every person employed in a rating as lifeboatman on any U.S. vessel requiring certificated lifeboatmen shall produce a certificate as lifeboatman or a merchant mariner's document (MMD) endorsed as lifeboatman or able seaman before signing articles of agreement. No certificate of efficiency as lifeboatman is required of any person employed on any unrigged vessel, except on a seagoing barge or on a tank barge navigating waters other than rivers and/or canals.

Service or training requirements. An applicant, to be eligible for certification as lifeboatman, must meet one of the following requirements:

1. At least 1 year of sea service in the deck department, or at least 2 years of sea service in the other departments of ocean, coastwise, Great Lakes, and other lakes, bays, or sounds vessels;

2. Graduation from a schoolship approved by and conducted under rules prescribed by the Commandant of the Coast Guard;

3. Satisfactory completion of basic training by a cadet of the U.S. Merchant Marine Cadet Corps;

4. Satisfactory completion of 3 years of training at the U.S. Naval Academy or the U.S. Coast Guard Academy, including two training cruises;

5. Satisfactory completion of a course of training approved by the Commandant and served aboard a training vessel;

6. Successful completion of a training course approved by the Commandant, such course to include a minimum of 30 hours of actual lifeboat training: *Provided,* that the applicant produces evidence of having served a minimum of 3 months at sea aboard ocean or coastwise vessels.

An applicant, to be eligible for certification as lifeboatman, shall be able to speak and understand the English language as would be required in the rating of lifeboatman and in an emergency aboard ship.

An applicant shall be 18 years old to be certified as proficient in survival craft under STCW Regulation VI/2.

Examination and demonstration of ability. Before a lifeboatman's endorsement may be granted, the applicant must prove to the satisfaction of the Coast Guard by oral or written examination and by actual demonstration that the applicant

1. Has been trained in all the operations connected with the launching of lifeboats and life rafts and the use of oars and sails;

2. Is acquainted with the practical handling of boats themselves; and,

3. Is capable of taking command of a boat's crew.

The oral or written examination is conducted in the English language and consists of seventy multiple-choice questions administered by the Coast Guard regarding:

1. Lifeboats and life rafts, the names of their essential parts, and a description of the required equipment;
2. The clearing away, swinging out, and lowering of lifeboats and life rafts; the handling of lifeboats under oars and sails, including questions relative to the proper handling of a boat in a heavy sea; and,
3. The operation and functions of commonly used types of davits.

The practical examination is a demonstration of ability that is normally conducted by the vessel master, but which may be witnessed by the Coast Guard Examining Officer, Coast Guard Marine Inspector, or a responsible person authorized in writing by the Officer in Charge, Marine Inspection. That person will sign a letter stating that the candidate has demonstrated ability in operations connected with the launching of lifeboats and life rafts including the carrying out of the usual orders given, in the practical handling of lifeboats, and in taking command of a lifeboat crew. The candidate may then present this letter to a Coast Guard Marine Inspection or Safety Office as evidence of satisfactory completion of all requirements and may be issued a merchant mariner's document endorsed for lifeboatman.

General provisions respecting merchant mariner's documents endorsed as lifeboatman. A merchant mariner's document endorsed as able seaman shall be considered as the equivalent of a certificate as lifeboatman or an endorsement as lifeboatman and it shall be accepted as a certificate as lifeboatman wherever required by law or regulation. However, when the holder documented as an able seaman has to be certificated as either proficient in survival craft and rescue boats or proficient in fast rescue boats, he or she shall hold an STCW endorsement.

Lifeboats

The following pages describe the lifesaving gear found on merchant vessels and set forth the methods for handling such equipment.

All lifeboats must have the ship's name and the number of the boat marked or painted on each bow in figures not less than 3 inches high (fig. 2). The top of thwarts, the lifeboat cover, side benches, and footings of lifeboats shall be painted or otherwise colored international orange. The area in way of the red mechanical disengaging gear control lever shall be painted or otherwise colored white to provide a contrasting background for the lever. This band of white should be approximately 12 inches wide, depending on the internal arrangement of the lifeboat. The oars, if provided, shall be conspicuously marked with the vessel's name. When there are lifeboats on both sides of the ship, odd numbers are given to the starboard boats and even numbers are given to the port boats. Lifeboat No. 1 will be the forward boat on the starboard side; lifeboat No. 2 will be the forward boat on the port side; lifeboat No. 3 will be next abaft lifeboat No. 1 on the

Fig. 2. Open lifeboat in gravity davits. Boat is secured for sea. Sea painter is rigged. Tricing pendant is clearly shown. Note that one end is secured to a padeye on the davit arm and the other to the MacCluney hook. A lifeboat may be constructed of galvanized steel, aluminum, or fiberglass.

starboard side; lifeboat No. 4 next abaft lifeboat No. 2 on the port side, etc. Under wartime or national emergency conditions the nesting of lifeboats can be authorized. In this event, the lifeboat under lifeboat No. 1 is numbered 1-A; the lifeboat under lifeboat No. 2 is numbered 2-A, etc. Nesting of lifeboats is not permitted under peacetime conditions.

The cubical contents and the number of persons allowed to be carried are also marked or painted on each lifeboat in letters or numbers not less than $1\frac{1}{2}$ inches high. In addition, the number of persons allowed shall be marked or painted on top of at least two thwarts in letters and numbers not less than 3 inches high. A builder's plate on the bow plating gives this and other information.

Open lifeboats similar to the drawing in figure 3 have been commonplace for many years and are still found on some domestic vessels and older vessels in foreign trade. Enclosed lifeboats are now the most common and required on all newer ships. All lifeboats are fitted with air tanks or built-in buoyancy compartments that will keep the boat afloat and not allow it to capsize when full of water and personnel.

A great deal of care has gone into the design and construction of lifeboats and *no changes should be made without the approval of the Coast Guard.* Only in an emergency may repairs be made without Coast Guard approval. Such repairs must be reported as soon as practicable to the Officer in Charge, Marine Inspection, in the first port of call after the repairs are made.

Lifeboats differ in their construction, but certain features are common to all. These features should be known because they are important in the handling and maintenance of these craft.

All lifeboats are built around a central keel usually made of heavy steel bar stock and connected to the stem and stern post. Older open boats were constructed of steel, aluminum, or fiberglass. Today, the enclosed boats are all made of fiberglass or improved forms of plastic with steel or other metal reinforcement. Enclosed boats are built similar to open boats with the *garboard* being the part of the hull next to the keel.

Fig. 3. An open lifeboat. This boat is fitted with rowlocks for oars and would have a sail. Boats of this type may also be fitted with hand-propelling equipment (flemming gear) or motorized.

The *gunwale* runs from stem to stern and is the top of the hull. The *sheer* is the part of the hull just below the gunwale. In open boats, the manual rudder is fitted with gudgeons and pintles and may be removed easily. The rudder on enclosed boats is remotely controlled by a wheel and is semiper-manently attached.

Near the turn of the *bilges, grab rails* are provided on the outside of the boat for persons to cling to should it overturn in the water. The grab rail is secured to small plates by fewer rivets than the number of rivets used to secure these plates in turn to the hull of the boat. If the grab rail should be torn off, the possibility of causing holes in the shell plating is re-duced by this method of attachment. Where there are no grab rails, knotted lines of 2-inch rope passed from gunwale to gunwale under the keel can serve as *grab lines* for the same purpose.

Where the lifeboat fits in the chocks, cradles, or against puddings, *doubler plating* is used. The doublers give added strength but are subject to wear and corrosion where the boat works in the chocks or against the puddings and should be examined when the boat is lifted or swung out. These areas require painting more frequently than other parts of a lifeboat's plating.

Aluminum lifeboats may be damaged by electrolytic corrosion if steel or some other metals are allowed in contact. Electrolysis may occur in a salt air atmosphere even if the dissimilar metals do not actually touch. No steel or iron tools should be left in aluminum boats. Enclosed boats are fitted with automatic and manual bilge pumps for removing water from the boat.

One or more drains are provided in each lifeboat to allow water to run out when the boat is out of the water. A small metal cage forms part of the drain extending below the shell of the boat. Within the cage, a rubber ball floats when the boat is in the water to act as an automatic closing valve. If there is rubbish in the cage, the ball cannot do its job. A cap is secured to each drain by a short length of small chain so it is ready for closing off the drain before the boat is launched. Drains should be kept clean at all times, the rubber ball should be in good condition, and *the drain cap should be screwed on before the boat is launched* (fig. 4).

On the bottom of the boat, or on the *floors* of larger boats, are placed the *bottom boards* or *footings*. These spread out the weight of persons or equipment over a wide area of the thin plating and contribute slightly to the strength of the boat. Footings are secured in a manner that allows them to be removed for painting or other maintenance work on the bottom of the boat.

The *thwarts* or seats extend from side to side in the boat. When the depth of the boat below the thwarts is *too* far for a rower's legs to reach the footings, foot rests or *stretchers* are provided. The thwarts are not only important as seats, they help to provide the athwartship strength of the boat in the

Fig. 4. One of the comparatively recent developments in lifesaving equipment is the enclosed lifeboat, shown here on Miranda gravity davits aboard *Chevron Mississippi.* It is constructed of fire retardant fiberglass and painted international orange. Sufficient buoyance is provided to make the boat unsinkable under all conditions up to a full load. A marine diesel fitted with a hydraulic gearbox can propel the boat at approximately 6.5 knots. Boats of this type may be equipped with complete life-support systems to allow operation in water covered with burning oil. Courtesy Watercraft America and W.B. Arnold Co., Inc.

same manner as the beams of a ship. Additional seating capacity is given by the *side benches.* Brackets from the gunwales help to stiffen and support the thwarts and side benches. If the boat is wide, upright stanchions are placed beneath the thwarts to help support the weight. The extreme forward seating is called the *bow sheets,* and the extreme after seating is called the *stern sheets.*

Provision tanks and *air tanks* for buoyancy are placed beneath the side benches and thwarts. Generally, such tanks are made so that they can be removed for painting and other maintenance work. Each tank is fitted with a small nipple so that its airtightness can be checked without removing it from the stowed position. This can be done with a small air pump or a short length of rubber tubing can be used to blow enough air through the nipple to cause the flat sides of most tanks to bulge if the tank is airtight. For very small leaks, the cap must be replaced when pressure is inside, as it would require some time for the leakage to be noticeable.

Seamen often can tell whether a tank is tight by observing it on a hot day. If the flat sides of any tank are not bulged like its neighboring tanks, there is a likelihood that it is leaking. When a tank holds air pressure, escaping air can be felt when the cap on the nipple is removed. Leaks can be located by brushing soapy water over the tank when there is air pressure inside. Bubbles will appear where the air is leaking out of the tank. Another method is to hold the tank under water so that escaping bubbles will reveal the leaks. *When tanks are removed for any purpose, they should be restowed in the original position.*

Unicellular plastic foam, polystyrene (Styrofoam), can be authorized to fill air tanks. This material, which consists of a plastic with a large number of small air cavities, will not absorb water, and will permit an air tank to be used that is no longer airtight. Enclosed boats rely on compartments built into the hull and filled with polystyrene foam (fig. 5).

A *mast hasp* and *step* are installed on each boat supplied with a sail. The step receives the bottom of the mast. The *hasp* is attached to a thwart and, assisted by the *wire stays,* holds the mast erect. A sail and mast are required in oar-propelled boats.

Many lifeboats are constructed with diesel engines. To avoid injuring people during drills, the deck area about the propeller should be kept clear. Motorboats have overboard openings in the shell for cooling water to enter, a clutch to permit idling the engine, and a reversing gear. Where the propeller shaft passes out of the *stern tube,* a *stern gland* prevents water from entering the boat. Fuel tanks for power-driven boats are built to keep danger from fire or explosion to a minimum, but care is necessary to keep open flames away from fuel or vapor that may be present. Motorboat engines must be operated each time abandon-ship drills are held, but unless the boat is put in the water, the lack of cooling water through the engine limits the time the engine can be run without overheating.

Hand-propelling gear is installed on some lifeboats. This type of propulsion has a propeller, stern tube, stern gland,

Fig. 5. Cutaway side view of enclosed lifeboat. Courtesy Watercraft America and W.B. Arnold Co., Inc.

and gears but instead of using an engine, power is furnished by pushing and pulling lever handles fore and aft. The bottom ends of the lever handles fit into sockets connected to a bar on each side of the boat. These two bars move cranks on the sides of the gear box near the boat's stern. Gear boxes on engine-driven as well as hand-propelled boats *must be kept free of water.* In cold weather this water can freeze and make it impossible for the gears to rotate and propel the boat. *The bars, cranks, and levers for hand-propelled boats must be kept clear when stowing gear.*

Whatever the means may be for propelling a lifeboat, as many of the crew as possible ought to be familiar with the method of operation. For motor-driven boats, the process of starting and stopping the engine, operating the clutch, reversing gear, and controlling speed should be known by all seamen who could be called on to operate the boat in an emergency.

Rudders are provided in every lifeboat for the purpose of controlling the direction the boats travel. Open boats have a rudder, usually made of wood, attached to the stern post by gudgeons and pintles. A tiller is attached to the rudder and is used by the operator of the lifeboat to move the rudder back and forth. Open boats are also equipped with a large oar that may be used in lieu of the rudder or if the rudder fails to maneuver the boat in tight situations. Enclosed boats require remote steering systems as there is no access to the rudder. Thus, a steering wheel is connected mechanically to the rudder that is connected to a rudder post or stern post directly behind the propeller.

Releasing gear is installed in lifeboats to let go the falls. Without such gear, letting go the falls in a seaway could be a difficult and dangerous job. The widely used Rottmer gear releases the falls at both ends of the boat at the same time. The person in charge of the boat turns a lever. This lever rotates shafting connected through universal joints to hook locks at both bow and stern ends of the boat. When the hook locks are opened, the hooks release the falls even though there may be weight on them.

While releasing gear helps to launch a boat safely in a seaway, its careless or unintentional use has led to serious accidents. Regulations require that the lever be painted red and marked: Danger—Lever Drops Boat. The person in charge of a boat must be sure that the crew knows that turning the lever at the wrong time can drop the boat from a height and seriously injure those in the boat. Regulations also provide that the top of thwarts, side benches, and footings of lifeboats shall be painted or otherwise colored international orange. The area in way of the red mechanical disengaging gear control lever shall be painted or otherwise colored white, to provide a contrasting background for the lever. This band of white should be approximately 12 inches wide, depending on the internal arrangement of the lifeboat. When crew are painting or working in boats hung on the davits, a wise precaution is to secure the boat independently of the falls with several turns of wire rope from the stem and stern post shackles to the davits.

The enclosed boats found on most new merchant ships have an improved releasing system (fig. 6). While the system works in a way similar to the Rottmer type, a lever is provided at the vessel operator station so the operator can release the boat directly. Further, the device is set up such that it can be armed to release as soon as the boat is afloat. It is also provided with a safety device that will not let the boat release under tension until it is afloat. A float interlock prevents the release device from operation until the water level floats the interlock. When the lever is moved to the release

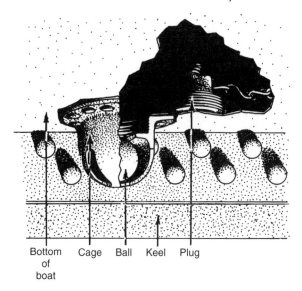

Bottom | Cage | Ball | Keel | Plug
of
boat

Fig. 6. Automatic lifeboat drain. Cap should be in place when boat is launched, although rubber ball will float and act as a check valve to keep water from entering boat. Drain must be kept clean and free from debris.

point, it will only release when it becomes afloat. The lever may be put into the override position only when the falls are not under tension, such as when you would like to set the boat on a dock.

Whenever the boat is in the water, it is good to work the releasing gear several times to see that it moves freely. At this time, note whether both hook locks open at the same time, as release of the bow fall before the stern fall with a ship underway could have serious consequences.

Rottmer-type releasing gear hooks are fitted with preventer bars (fig. 7). These bars prevent the falls from accidentally becoming detached when the boat is waterborne, when there is no weight on the falls.

Because the task of getting a boat and its complement safely in and out of the water is the most hazardous part of

Fig. 7. Rottmer releasing gear. As the red-painted release lever is tripped on orders of the boat commander, the universal joint rotates. This forces the hook to move in the "up" position, and the boat is freed from the falls. Prior to recovery the release lever must be rotated back to its normal position so that the boat can once again be "hooked" onto the falls.

lifeboat handling, considerable attention has been given to the releasing gear. It is a helpful device in competent hands, but if it is entrusted to an untrained individual, it could be misused and cause a serious accident.

Sec. 199.175 Survival craft and rescue boat equipment.

(a) All lifeboat and rescue boat equipment—

(1) Must be secured within the boat by lashings, by storage in lockers or compartments, by storage in brackets or similar mounting arrangements, or by other suitable means;

(2) Must be secured in such a manner as not to interfere with any abandonment procedures or reduce seating capacity;

(3) Must be as small and of as little mass as possible;

(4) Must be packed in a suitable and compact form; and

(5) Should be stowed so the items do not—

(i) Reduce the seating capacity;

(ii) Adversely affect the seaworthiness of the survival craft or rescue boat; or

(iii) Overload the launching appliance.

(b) Each lifeboat, rigid liferaft, and rescue boat, unless otherwise stated in this paragraph, must carry the equipment listed in this paragraph and specified for it in table 199.175 of this section under the vessel's category of service. A lifeboat that is also a rescue boat must carry the equipment in the table column marked for a lifeboat.

(1) *Bailer.* The bailer must be buoyant.

(2) *Bilge pump.* The bilge pump must be approved under approval series 160.044 and must be installed in a ready-to-use condition as follows:

(i) The bilge pump for a lifeboat approved for less than 70 persons must be either size 2 or size 3.

(ii) The bilge pump for a lifeboat approved for 70 persons or more must be size 3.

(3) *Boathook.* In the case of a boat launched by falls, the boathook must be kept free for fending-off purposes. For inflated rescue boats and for rigid-inflated rescue boats, each boathook must be designed to minimize the possibility of damage to the inflated portions of the hull.

(4) *Bucket.* The bucket must be made of corrosion-resistant material and should either be buoyant or have an attached lanyard at least 1.8 meters (6 feet) long.

(5) *Can opener.* A can opener may be in a jackknife approved under approval series 160.043.

(6) *Compass.* The compass and its mounting arrangement must be approved under approval series 160.014. In a totally enclosed lifeboat, the compass must be permanently fitted at the steering position; in any other boat it must be provided with a binnacle, if necessary to protect it from the weather, and with suitable mounting arrangements.

(7) *Dipper.* The dipper must be rustproof and attached to a lanyard that should be at least 0.9 meters (3 feet) long.

(8) *Drinking cup.* The drinking cup must be graduated and rustproof. The cup should also be of a breakage-resistant material.

(9) *Fire extinguisher.* The fire extinguisher must be approved under approval series 162.028. The fire extinguisher must be type B-C, size II, or larger. Two type B-C, size I fire extinguishers may be carried in place of a type B-C, size II fire extinguisher.

(10) *First aid kit.* The first aid kit in a lifeboat and in a rescue boat must be approved under approval series 160.041. The first aid kit in a rigid liferaft must be approved under approval series 160.054.

(11) *Fishing kit.* The fishing kit must be approved under approval series 160.061.

(12) *Flashlight.* The flashlight must be a type I or type III that is constructed and marked in accordance with the American Society of Testing and Materials (ASTM) F 1014 (incorporated by reference, see Sec. 199.05). One spare set of batteries and one spare bulb, stored in a watertight container, must be provided for each flashlight.

(13) *Hatchet.* The hatchet must be approved under approval series 160.013. The hatchet should be stowed in brackets near the release mechanism and, if more than one hatchet is carried, the hatchets should be stowed at opposite ends of the boat.

(14) *Heaving line.* The heaving line must be buoyant, must be at least 30 meters (99 feet) long, must have a buoy-

ant rescue quoit attached to one end, and should be at least 8 millimeters ($\frac{5}{16}$ inches) in diameter.

(15) *Instruction card.* The instruction card must be waterproof and contain the information required by IMO Resolution A.657(16). The instruction card should be located so that it can be easily seen upon entering the liferaft.

(16) *Jackknife.* The jackknife must be approved under approval series 160.043 and must be attached to the boat by its lanyard.

(17) *Knife.* The knife must be of the non-folding type with a buoyant handle as follows:

(i) The knife for a rigid liferaft must be secured to the raft by a lanyard and stowed in a pocket on the exterior of the canopy near the point where the painter is attached to the liferaft. If an approved jackknife is substituted for the second knife required on a liferaft equipped for 13 or more persons, the jackknife must also be secured to the liferaft by a lanyard.

(ii) The knife in an inflated or rigid-inflated rescue boat must be of a type designed to minimize the possibility of damage to the fabric portions of the hull.

(18) *Ladder.* The boarding ladder must be capable of being used at each entrance on either side or at the stern of the boat to enable persons in the water to board the boat. The lowest step of the ladder must be not less than 0.4 meters (15.75 inches) below the boat's light waterline.

(19) *Mirror.* The signalling mirror must be approved under approval series 160.020 (fig. 8).

(20) *Oars and paddles.* Each lifeboat and rescue boat must have buoyant oars or paddles of the number, size, and type specified by the manufacturer of the boat. An oarlock or equivalent device, either permanently installed or attached to the boat by a lanyard or chain, must be provided for each oar. Each oar should have the vessel's name marked on it in block letters (fig. 9).

(21) *Painter.*

(i) One painter on a lifeboat and the painter on a rescue boat must be attached by a painter release device at the forward end of the lifeboat. The second painter on a lifeboat must be secured at or near the bow of the lifeboat, ready for

Fig. 8. Sighting a rear-sight-type signaling mirror.

use. On lifeboats to be launched by free-fall launching, both painters must be stowed near the bow ready for use (fig. 10).

(A) If the painter is of synthetic material, the painter must be of a dark color or certified by the manufacturer to be resistant to deterioration from ultraviolet light.

(B) The painter for a lifeboat and each painter for a rescue boat must be of a length that is at least twice the distance from the stowage position of the boat to the waterline with

Fig. 9. Parts of an oar.

the vessel in its lightest seagoing condition, or must be 15 meters (50 feet) long, whichever is the greater.

(C) The painter must have a breaking strength of at least 34 kiloNewtons (7,700 pounds-force).

(ii) The painter for a rigid liferaft must be of a length that is at least 20 meters (66 feet) plus the distance from the liferaft's stowed position to the waterline with the vessel in its lightest seagoing condition, or must be 15 meters (50 feet) long, whichever is the greater.

(A) If the painter is of synthetic material, the painter must be of a dark color or certified by the manufacturer to be resistant to deterioration from ultraviolet light.

(B) The painter must have a breaking strength of at least 15 kiloNewtons (3,937 pounds-force) for liferafts approved for more than 25 persons, of at least 20 kiloNewtons (2,250 pounds-force) for liferafts approved for 9 to 25 persons, and of

Fig. 10. A sea painter.

at least 7.5 kiloNewtons (1,687 pounds-force) for any other liferaft.

(C) The painter must have a float-free link meeting the requirements of part 160, subpart 160.073 of this chapter secured to the end of the painter that is attached to the vessel. The float-free link arrangement must break under a load of 2.2 ± 0.4 kiloNewtons (400 to 536 pounds-force).

(22) *Provisions.* Each unit of provisions must be approved under approval series 160.046 and must provide at least 10,000 kiloJoules (2,390 calories). Individual provision packages may provide less than 10,000 kiloJoules, as long as the total quantity of provisions on board provides for at least 10,000 kiloJoules per person.

(23) *Pump.* The pump or bellows must be manually operated and should be arranged so it is capable of inflating any part of the inflatable structure of the rescue boat.

(24) *Radar reflector.* The radar reflector must be capable of detection at a distance of 4 nautical miles and must have a mounting arrangements to install it on the boat in its proper orientation. A 9- GigaHertz radar transponder may be substituted for the radar reflector if the transponder is accepted by the Federal Communications Commission as meeting the requirements of 47 CFR part 80 and is stowed in the boat or raft.

(25) *Rainwater collection device.* The rainwater collection device must be arranged to collect falling rain and direct it into the water tanks in the lifeboat. If the lifeboat carries a manually-powered, reverse osmosis desalinator approved under approval series 160.058, a rainwater collection device is not required.

(26) *Repair kit.* The repair kit for an inflated and a rigid-inflated rescue boat must be packed in a suitable container and include at least—

(i) Six sealing clamps;

(ii) Five 50-millimeter (2-inch) diameter tube patches;

(iii) A roughing tool; and

(iv) A container of cement compatible with the tube fabric. The cement must have an expiration date on its container that is not more than 24 months after the date of manufacture of the cement.

(27) *Sea anchor* (fig. 11).

(i) The sea anchor for a lifeboat must be approved under approval series 160.019.

(ii) Each sea anchor for a rigid liferaft must be of the type specified by the liferaft manufacturer and must be fitted with a shock resistant hawser. It may also be fitted with a tripping line. One sea anchor must be permanently attached to the liferaft in such a way that, when the liferaft is waterborne, it will cause the liferaft to lie oriented to the wind in the most stable manner. The second sea anchor must be stowed in the liferaft as a spare. A davit-launched liferaft and a liferaft on a passenger vessel must have the permanently attached sea anchor arranged to deploy automatically when the liferaft floats free.

(iii) The sea anchor for a rescue boat must be of the type specified by the rescue boat manufacturer, and must have a hawser of adequate strength that is at least 10 meters (33 feet) long.

(28) *Searchlight.*

(i) The searchlight must be of the type originally provided with the approved lifeboat or rescue boat, or must be certified by the searchlight manufacturer to meet ASTM F 1003

Fig. 11. A lifeboat sea anchor.

(incorporated by reference, see Sec. 199.05). The boat must carry two spare bulbs.

(ii) The searchlight must be permanently mounted on the canopy or must have a stanchion-type or collapsible-type, portable mounting on the canopy. The mounting must be located to enable operation of the searchlight by the boat operator.

(iii) The searchlights power source must be capable of operating the light without charging or recharging for not less than—

(A) Three hours of continuous operation; or

(B) Six hours total operation when it is operated in cycles of 15 minutes on and 5 minutes off.

(iv) If the searchlight's power source is an engine starting battery, there must be sufficient battery capacity to start the engine at the end of either operating period specified in paragraph (b)(28)(iii) of this section.

(v) The searchlight's power source must be connected to the searchlight using watertight electrical fittings.

(29) *Seasickness kit.* The seasickness kit must be in a waterproof package and must include one waterproof seasickness bag, anti-seasickness medication sufficient for one person for 48 hours, and instructions for using the medication. Each seasickness kit should be stowed within reach of the seat for which it is intended.

(30) *Signal, smoke.* The smoke signal must be approved under approval series 160.122.

(31) *Signal, hand flare.* The hand flare must be approved under approval series 160.121.

(32) *Signal, rocket parachute flare.* The rocket parachute flare must be approved under approval series 160.136.

(33) *Skates and fenders.* The skates and fenders must be as specified by the lifeboat or rescue boat manufacturer to facilitate launching and prevent damage to a lifeboat intended for launching down the side of a vessel.

(34) *Sponge.* The sponge must be suitable for soaking up water.

(35) *Survival instructions.* The survival instructions must be as described in IMO Resolution A.657(16), Annex I for liferafts and Annex II for lifeboats.

(36) *Table of lifesaving signals.* The table of lifesaving signals must be as described in Annex IV to the International Regulations for Preventing Collisions at Sea 1972, as amended, and must be printed on a waterproof card or stored in a waterproof container.

(37) *Thermal protective aid.* The thermal protective aid must be approved under approval series 160.174.

(38) *Tool kit.* The tool kit must contain sufficient tools for minor adjustments to the engine and its accessories.

(39) *Towline.* The towline must be buoyant and at least 50 meters (164 feet) long. The towline must have a breaking strength of not less than 13.3 kiloNewtons (3,000 pounds-force) or be of sufficient strength to tow the largest liferaft carried on the vessel when loaded with its full complement of persons and equipment at a speed of at least 2 knots.

(40) *Water.* The water must be emergency drinking water approved under approval series 160.026.

(i) The requirement for up to one-third of the emergency drinking water may be met by a desalting apparatus approved under approval series 160.058 that is capable of producing the substituted amount of water in 2 days.

(ii) The requirement for up to two-thirds of the emergency drinking water may be met by a manually-powered, reverse osmosis desalinator approved under approval series 160.058 and that is capable of producing the substituted amount of water in 2 days.

(41) *Whistle.* The whistle must be corrosion-resistant, and should be a ball-type or multi-tone whistle that is attached to a lanyard.

TABLE 199.175—SURVIVAL CRAFT EQUIPMENT

Item No.	Item	International Voyage			Short International Voyage		
		Lifeboat	Rigid Liferaft (SOLAS A pack)	Rescue Boat	Lifeboat	Rigid Liferaft (SOLAS B pack)	Rescue Boat
1	Bailer[1]	1	1	1	1	1	1
2	Bilge pump[2]	1	—	—	1	—	—
3	Boathook	2	—	1	2	—	1
4	Bucket[3]	2	—	1	2	—	1
5	Can opener	3	3	—	3	—	—
6	Compass	1	—	1	1	—	1
7	Dipper	1	—	—	1	—	—
8	Drinking cup	1	1	—	1	—	—

9	Fire extinguisher	1	—	1	1	—	1
10	First aid kit	1	1	1	1	1	1
11	Fishing kit	1	1	—	—	—	—
12	Flashlight	1	1	1	1	1	1
13	Hatchet	2	—	—	2	—	—
14	Heaving line	2	1	2	2	1	2
15	Instruction card	—	1	—	—	1	—
16	Jackknife	1	—	—	1	—	—
17	Knife[1][4]	—	1	1	—	1	1
18	Ladder	1	—	1	1	—	1
19	Mirror, signaling	1	1	—	1	1	—
20	Oars, units[5][6]	1	—	1	1	—	1
	Paddles	—	2	—	—	2	—
21	Painter	2	1	1	2	1	1
22	Provisions (units per person)	1	1	—	—	—	—
23	Pump[7]	—	—	1	—	—	1
24	Radar reflector	1	1	1	1	1	1
25	Rainwater collection device	1	—	—	1	—	—
26	Repair kit[7]	—	—	1	—	—	1
27	Sea anchor	1	2	1	1	2	1
28	Searchlight	1	—	1	1	—	1
29	Seasickness kit (units per person)	1	1	—	1	1	—
30	Signal, smoke	2	2	—	2	1	—
31	Signal, hand flare	6	6	—	6	3	—
32	Signal, parachute flare	4	4	—	4	2	—
33	Skates and fenders[8]	1	—	1	1	—	1
34	Sponge[7]	—	2	2	—	2	2
35	Survival instructions	1	1	—	1	1	—
36	Table of lifesaving signals	1	1	—	1	1	—
37	Thermal protective aids[9]	10%	10%	10%	10%	10%	10%
38	Tool kit	1	—	—	1	—	—
39	Towline[10]	1	—	1	1	—	1
40	Water (liters per person)	3	1.5	—	3	—	—
41	Whistle	1	1	1	1	1	1

Notes:

[1] Each liferaft equipped for 13 persons or more must carry two of these items.

[2] Not required for boats of self-bailing design.

[3] Not required for inflated or rigid-inflated rescue boats.

[4] A hatchet counts towards this requirement in rigid rescue boats.

[5] Oars are not required on a free-fall lifeboat; a unit of oars means the number of oars specified by the boat manufacturer.

[6] Rescue boats may substitute buoyant paddles for oars, as specified by the manufacturer.

[7] Not required for a rigid rescue boat.

[8] Required if specified by the boat manufacturer.

[9] Sufficient thermal protective aids are required for at least 10% of the persons the survival craft is equipped to carry, but not less than two.

[10] Required only if the lifeboat is also the rescue boat.

[CGD 84-069, 61 FR 25313, May 20, 1996; 61 FR 40281, Aug. 1, 1996; 63 FR 52819, Oct. 1. 1998; USCG-1999-6216, 64 FR 53229, Oct. 1, 1999; USCG-2000-7790, 65 FR 58465, Sept. 29, 2000]

Davits, Winches, Blocks, and Falls

Although there may be a few exceptions that allow the use of other gear, in all normal circumstances davits are required aboard merchant vessels for the lowering and hoisting of lifeboats. Davits are installed in pairs and can be extended over the water from the side of the ship in order to lower or hoist the lifeboat by means of wire rope or fiber falls that are attached to the heads of the davit arms.

There are three general types of davits: radial or round bar, mechanical, and gravity. A further development of the gravity davit is the Miranda gravity davit, especially designed for use with enclosed lifeboats.

Although the older radial and mechanical davits are rarely found on modern merchant ships, a description of them must be given because these davits are still used for other purposes on the ship:

Radial davits. In moving the boat from the inboard to the outboard position, the heads of the davit arms swing in horizontal arcs and do not raise or lower as do the heads of the other davit types. The boat is swung aft until the bow clears the forward davit arm; then the boat is swung outboard and forward to the lowering position. Hand turning-out gears may be attached to each davit arm to ensure that the boat can be swung outboard when the ship is listing heavily. Though radial davits are easily designed and manufactured, the difficulty of swinging out a heavy boat with these davits prevents their use on large ships. Only small vessels are allowed to carry radial davits (fig. 12).

Mechanical davits. The two common mechanical davits are the sheath screw and the quadrantal davits. These two types may be further described by terms that refer to the shape of the davit arm, either straight boom or crescent (figs. 13, 14, and 15[A]). For all types, the davit arm is cranked out by screws, gears, or other mechanical means, and it moves outboard in a plane that is perpendicular to the side of the ship.

Gravity davits. Gravity davits have been required on all new construction merchant ships for a number of years.

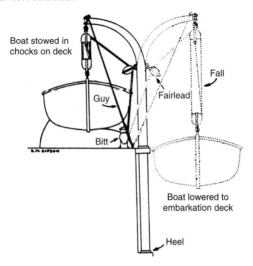

Fig. 12. A radial or round bar davit. Radial davits have not been installed in new construction ships in the American merchant marine for many years. They require a considerable number of men to launch or recover a lifeboat. They may still be seen occasionally on smaller vessels or yachts.

Although there are several types, all of them depend upon gravity to launch the boat (fig. 15[B]). Power is not used except when raising the boat. After the release of the locking bars, these davits move from the inboard to the outboard position with no application of force except that which is needed to lift the winch brake handle. The most common gravity davit consists of two davit arms that ride on rollers down fixed trackways to the outboard position. Another type is pivoted at the lower ends of both davit arms, which move outboard through a system of mechanical linkages. One person, who must remain aboard ship, can lower a lifeboat from the secured position to the water. Gravity davits are required for larger lifeboats. The most recent developments are the Miranda gravity davit and the pivot gravity davit, which are especially designed for the use of enclosed lifeboats. Miranda-type davits are common on all new

Fig. 13. A sheath screw boom davit. Sheath screw and quadrantal davits (shown in fig. 15[A]), are also called mechanical davits, and are an improvement on the original radial davit. The sheath screw boom and sheath screw crescent davit (fig. 14) operate in exactly the same way. While no longer used for lifesaving installations, these davits are easier to use than radial davits and often are used for work boats.

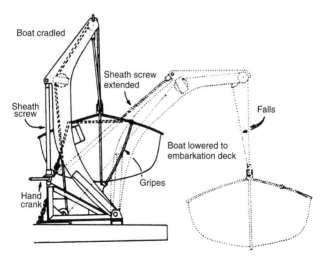

Fig. 14. A sheath screw crescent davit.

Fig. 15. (A) a quadrantal davit and (B) a gravity davit.

(A)

(B)

Fig. 16. (A) A Miranda gravity davit. Miranda davits are designed for use with enclosed lifeboats. Figure 4 shows the installation of a Miranda davit. (B) The pivot gravity davit, which has one pivot point for each arm. The falls are led between the davits via a crossbeam, leaving the deck clear of wire. The boat is stowed in such a way as to leave the deck beneath clear. Courtesy W.B. Arnold Co., Inc.

construction. These davits are illustrated in figure 16(A) and (B). On both installations, the lifeboat commander can lower the boat from the embarkation deck to water from his position in the boat itself. Both davit installations and launching procedures vary depending upon the time period when the davits were installed, as well as any modifications that may have been necessary to fit them to their parent ship. Enclosed lifeboats launched with Miranda-type davits normally have an interlock that requires that the boat be in the water before it can be released from the falls. Consequently, it is extremely important to be completely familiar with the launching procedures posted by the davits as well as by the coxswain's console in the lifeboat. The prudent seaman will never be dependent on someone else to teach him something in an emergency that he should have learned ahead of time.

Boat falls. With radial davits, fiber rope falls are used, but on gravity davits, wire is always employed. Mechanical davits use either wire or rope.

Fiber rope falls are rove through blocks at the ends of the davits and at the ends of the boat for the mechanical advantage and increased strength afforded by multiple parts. The boats are lowered by paying out the rope over cruciform bitts or cleats provided for the purpose.

Fiber rope is stowed on reels or coiled in boxes. These should be covered to keep off ice and snow, and to protect the rope from exposure to the weather. Good operating practice with Manila or synthetic fall is to "end for end" them after one year, i.e., reverse the lead of the falls to ensure more even wear, and to renew them after two years. The replaced rope can be used for less critical purposes than lifesaving equipment.

Wire rope falls are handled from a winch. An automatic brake limits the lowering speed, while a hand brake gives manual control of lowering. Wire rope falls must be replaced every four years with certified wire rope. Motor or hand power is used for hoisting these falls, which must be kept coated with a grease that provides lubrication for the internal working of the wire as well as protection against corrosion.

Blocks for both wire and fiber rope must be kept well greased and working easily. An important duty of the crew at lifeboat drills is to see that sheaves for blocks and fairleads work freely.

The decks on which lifeboats are carried must be kept clear of freight or anything else that would interfere with the immediate launching of the lifeboat.

The use of gravity-type davits with electric motor-driven winches has simplified rapid lifeboat launching and hoisting. These almost automatic davits require increased care and skill in their maintenance and routine inspection. Special points to be noted are as follows:

1. Limit switches—Before hoisting the boats into the stowed position, check the operation of these devices by pushing down the lever arm to see whether the winch motor stops. Limit switches are in the control or power circuit for the motor. An emergency disconnect switch, which can stop flow of all power to the winch motor, must be manned when the boat is hoisted. Shipmasters must inspect limit switches and emergency disconnect switches every three months. Electric motors for lifeboat winches are powerful enough to easily break the wire rope falls if the motor is used to pull up the davit against the stops. This same casualty can occur if air-actuated equipment is used to hoist the davit against the stops. For this reason, the davits should be hand cranked for the last 12 inches or more to their final stowed position.

2. Winches—Unless the lubrication schedule for winches is faithfully followed, moisture can accumulate in the winch enclosures to damage wiring and freeze gears in cold weather, preventing the boat from being lowered. Covers should be fitted over winches to keep ice and snow from freezing on the wire falls (fig. 17).

3. Hand cranks—Winch hand cranks have couplings that automatically disengage the crank if the electric motor starts to turn the winch. In order to further reduce any possibility of injury, the emergency disconnect switch should always be in the off position when men arc hand cranking.

Fig. 17. Lifeboat winch controls.

Lifeboat Operations

Launching. The most difficult operation in handling life-boats is launching, including embarkation of passengers and crew. To achieve this safely and efficiently, frequent drills are necessary so that each crew member learns his or her duties and the order in which they must be performed. Training should be so thorough that the crew performs correctly despite any confusion or excitement. For these reasons, weekly drills are required by U.S. laws. U.S. ships are built to resist damage in an accident. The captain may deem it best for all hands to stay aboard for their own safety and that of the ship. Don't abandon ship before orders are given by the captain or ship's officers.

When using boats handled by mechanical davits, the following would represent a typical sequence of operations necessary to swing the boat over the side:

1. Remove lifeboat cover and its supporting ridgepole. Put cap on drain. Lead sea painter forward, and make fast outboard and clear of all obstructions.
2. Release outboard gripes first so the crew member assigned to this task cannot be knocked over the side by the swinging of the boat.

3. With falls taut and secured to cleats, cruciform bitts, or winches, release inboard gripes and keel locking lug on chocks.
4. The davits with the boat suspended may now be swung out. Chocks are built high enough above the deck so that if the falls are taut, no hoisting of the boat to clear the deck edge is necessary.
5. When the boat is in outboard position, lower to embarkation deck. With mechanical davits, it is often desirable to swing the davits back inboard so that the boat can be frapped-in snug. This will allow persons to get in the boat without jumping any space between boat and deck.
6. If the ship is pitching as well as rolling, frapping lines should have a fore and aft as well as thwartships lead. With boat complement aboard, davits are again swung outboard. Frapping lines are eased as necessary, and the boat lowered away on falls. In rough weather, the boat crew may have to fend off from ship's side as the ship rolls, and fenders made of mattresses or other available material can be used to cushion impacts.
7. When the boat is in the water, the lifeboatman in charge should turn the releasing gear. The boat can then be held alongside with painter so that crew members who remained aboard to lower can climb down a ladder into the boat to abandon ship. If the boat cannot be kept alongside because of rough weather, these crew members can throw heaving lines to the boat; then, with one end secured to themselves, they can get into the water and be pulled aboard the boat.

For boats handled by gravity davits, a different sequence is necessary. This is as follows:

1. Remove boat cover and its supporting ridgepole. Put cap on drain. Lead sea painter forward, and make fast outboard and clear of all obstructions.
2. Release gripes.
3. Raise winch brake handle, and davits with suspended boat should roll to the outboard position. Lower away to

embarkation deck. The tricing lines will bring the boat
to the side of the ship. The brake should be put on before
the tricing lines take all the weight.

4. Before passengers and crew enter the boat at the embarkation deck, frapping lines should be passed and hove
taut. With all aboard the boat seated, the hooks on the
tricing wires should be released and the boat eased outboard by slacking frapping lines. Releasing the tricing
wires without observing these precautions will allow the
boat to swing out violently, risking a spill of occupants
over the side (fig. 18).

On some U.S.-flag ships that were built in foreign
countries, bowsing tackles may be used instead of frapping lines. These accomplish the same purpose as frapping lines, but are tended from the lifeboat rather than
from the embarkation deck of the parent ship. Frequently, two-fold purchases are used. The advantage is
that only the brakeman need remain aboard ship when
the lifeboat is launched. The disadvantage is that bowsing tackles are cumbersome, and more gear must be
stowed in the lifeboat.

5. With the boat in the outboard position, it may be lowered
into the water and released. The remaining sequence is
similar to that for boats lowered by mechanical davits.

The launching of enclosed boats in Miranda-type davits is
quite simple. At the entry point of the boat, a preventer release is provided. This will need to be released before entry
into the boat so the boat can be lowered from inside. Load the
passengers and crew and strap them in. Place the release
lever into the ready position, and pull the lowering wire. The
boat will lower to the water and release when in the water.

Picking up a boat at sea can present as many problems as
launching it. It is best done by maneuvering to place the boat
ahead and to leeward of the ship with the wind about broad
on the bow of the ship. If the ship now overtakes the boat
with both making way through the water on parallel courses,
a sea painter can be passed to the boat. After the painter is
fast, the boat's propeller is stopped or oars boated, and then

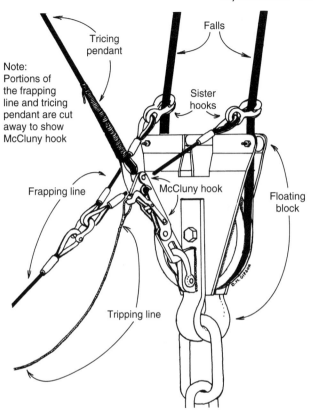

Fig. 18. Tricing pendant and frapping line.

the boat is brought alongside with rudder or steering oar. The ship can make slow way through the water. If the sea painter is secured well abaft the stem, the tendency to sheer off can be overcome by a strap about the painter from the stem hove close. After the falls are hooked and the boat is hoisted clear of the water, most of the crew can climb the ladder and get aboard the ship; those remaining in the boat should grip the manropes for safety.

On boats handled with gravity davits, the boat is hoisted to a position where the tricing lines can be made fast. It is next lowered to the embarkation deck where crew in the boat can get out. It is then brought up to the stowed position, using the hand cranks for the last 12 inches or more. When the boat is back in the stowed position, crew can get back in the boat to pass the gripes, replace the ridgepole and cover, and make the boat again secured for sea.

Commands for boats under oars. Commands for boats under oars have not undergone change for many years. A seaman of 100 years ago would be at home in a boat today.

While most commands are addressed to both banks of oars, it may often happen that the coxswain desires to give the command only to one bank, or to give one command to one bank and another command to the other. For example, if it is desired to bring the boat about quickly the coxswain may do so by giving the command "give way" to the port bank and "starboard back" to the starboard bank. In any case, it is good policy to call the *bank* first, followed by the command, rather than calling the command followed by the bank that is to execute it. Otherwise one bank may begin to execute a command that is not addressed to it.

When one bank of oars is executing one command and the other bank another, and it is desired to give them a command that will apply to both, call "oars" first. This cancels the preceding command and gives both banks an opportunity to start the new order in unison.

Give new commands at the beginning of the stroke, *not* at the end. This gives the oars an opportunity to complete the stroke and execute the new command in unison. The commands and how to execute them are as follows:

1. Stand by the oars—Stroke oar ships his rowlock, clears his oar, and lays it on the gunwale, handle shoved forward to proper position. Immediately, each man back of the stroke oar does the same thing, keeping his oar *inboard* of the oar in front of him.

2. Out oars—Usually given after the command, "Stand by the oars." Oars are placed in rowlocks in the same position as for "oars."

3. Up oars—The oars are tossed quickly to a vertical position, blades trimmed in a fore-and-aft plane and in line with that of the stroke oar, handles of oars resting on bottom boards, outboard hand grasping loom of oar at height of chin, wrist of inboard arm resting on inboard thigh and steadying oar.

4. Toss oars—Complete the stroke and come to "up oars" position. The difference in meaning between this command and "up oars" has disappeared with the passing of time.

5. Shove off—Inboard bowman shoves off smartly from the ship's side with boat hook using the blunt end, shoving the boat ahead, if possible. Outboard bowman takes in the painter. Coxswain sheers off and hauls ahead on the stanchions of the gangway or on the grab rope, assisted as necessary by the inboard stroke oar. Fenders are rigged in by men abreast of them. Bowmen place boat hooks fore and aft, seat themselves, and get their oars ready.

6. Let fall—Given when the boat is clear of the ship's side. As the boat sheers off and away from the ship, it may be necessary to let fall the forward oars before there is room for the after oars to clear the ship's side. This would be done by the command "1, 2, and 3 let fall," or "2 and 3 let fall." Other oars remain vertical until the command "Let fall." At this command all oars are dropped, blades outboard, into the rowlock. Slip the inboard hand to the handle and come to the position "Oars" with both hands on the handle. Under no circumstances should the blades dip water in letting fall.

7. Give way together—All oarsmen take a full stroke, keeping cadence with the stroke oar, *by watching the back of the person in front of them.* Feathering of the oar should become habitual and automatic. If stroke oars have not been able to get their oars out in position by the time the command "give way together" has been given, they will do so quickly and take up the stroke. Continue to pull a strong, steady stroke, using the back, and maintain silence.

8. Hold water—This command is given when way is on the boat and a quick stop is desired. Drop the blades in the water vertically and hold them perpendicular to the keel line. If considerable way is on, especially in a boat that is heavily loaded, care must be used in holding water, or the force of it may carry away the rowlock, gunwale, or the oar itself. Under these conditions, drop the oar in the water at a slight angle, top forward, allowing the water to "slip," and gradually bring the blade vertical as way is lost.

9. Port, hold water (starboard, hold water)—If the boat is underway and the oars rowing, a quick turn may be made by giving this command to one side only, the other side continuing with the command "give way."

10. Stern all—When rowing in ahead motion, complete the stroke, then commence to back water, gradually increasing the depth of immersion of the blades.

11. Back water—Row in astern motion. The difference in meaning between the commands "stern all" and "back water," if any, is now lost with the passage of time. In any event, a good coxswain or boat commander should always give as much warning as possible before giving a new command. The boat commander can do this by giving the command, "oars," and then giving the command, "back water." If the boat has any way at all, it is good seamanship to give the command "hold water" first to help take way off the boat. Going from ahead to astern without warning may result in broken rowlocks or rowlocks popped out of their sockets. Sometimes the command "port back water" or "starboard back water" is used when it is desired to come about quickly or turn in close quarters. When this is done the other side can either hold water or give way together.

12. Trail oars—Used in passing obstructions in which the span of the oars would make passing difficult. This command is given when the oars are in the water. Finish the stroke, release the handle of the oar, allowing it to draw fore-and-aft and trail alongside. This command is somewhat awkward to execute, and the oarsman must be careful not to lose his oar. If the boat is in danger of being set down on a dock or other obstruction, oars on that side should be boated to protect them from damage.

13. Bank oars—Used to enable oarsmen to rest their arms when laying to and the position of "oars" would be tiresome to hold. Draw the oar through the rowlock until the handle rests on the opposite gunwale. It is given from the command "oars." The command, "oars across the boat" is sometimes used instead of "bank oars."

14. In bows—Given as landing is approached and while the blades are in the water. Bowmen complete the stroke, toss oars and boat them, seize boat hooks, stand erect in bow, facing forward, holding boat hooks vertical in front of them until they are needed.

15. Way enough—Given as the boat approaches for a landing, and takes the place of the two commands "oars" and "boat oars." The command is given at the beginning of a stroke. The stroke is completed, oars tossed to about a 45° angle and boated, forward oar first, stroke oar last. Unship the rowlock. This command may be unnecessary, but can be used to advantage by a good boat commander and a well-trained boat crew.

16. Oars—To stop pulling. Given when the coxswain estimates that the boat's headway will carry her to the landing, and while the blades are in the water. Complete the stroke and bring the oars horizontal, at right angles to the keel, blades feathered.

17. Boat the oars—Toss the blades to a 45° angle, and lay them inside the boat, blades forward, forward oar first, stroke oar last. Unship the rowlock.

The lifeboat waterborne. After the lifeboat is in the water and the passengers and crew embarked, it is of utmost importance to get the boat clear of the side of the ship as soon as possible. Even in comparatively calm weather the boat can be damaged or personnel injured if the boat stays alongside. If the ship has way on, the boat will clear the side by riding on the sea painter which can then be cast off. If the ship is dead in the water, it may be necessary to fend off by the use of boat hooks or oars. Ensure that none of the lines hanging over the side of the vessel foul the propeller or any other part of the boat.

Once clear of the side of the ship, the lifeboat should remain in the vicinity to ensure that all survivors are picked up. In the modern day it is extremely unlikely that a ship could sink without shore stations being informed. All ships are now equipped with an EPIRB (Emergency Position-Indicating Radio Beacon), which will float free of the sinking ship and start transmitting signals when the ship goes down. This ensures that your position will be known even though the radio officer has not had time to send an SOS. As a consequence, rescue ships or aircraft will know the ship's position if survivors stay near the scene of the shipwreck.

The lifeboatman in charge of a boat should try to keep morale high and to make people in the boat as comfortable as possible. Signaling equipment should be ready and used when rescue vessels are sighted or known to be in the vicinity. Metal objects hoisted as high as possible will help radar-equipped rescue ships to locate the lifeboat.

Since position is probably known and rescue operations will shortly be underway, undertaking a long ocean voyage to the nearest land should be considered only under the most dire circumstances. Motor lifeboats have fuel only for 24 hours. Attempting to sail or row for a long distance is foolhardy. Modern lifeboats are seaworthy, but they are not meant for sailing. Most of the great lifeboat voyages in history, such as that of Captain Bligh of *Bounty* fame, were made in warm water with favorable trade winds helping the boat towards its destination. In that era, radio, aircraft, and modern search and rescue procedures were unknown.

Handling propeller-driven boats. Most newer ships are equipped with either motor-propelled lifeboats or boats fitted with hand propelling equipment that turns a propeller. A few merchant ships and all navy ships have diesel utility boats. The fundamentals of boat handling are much the same whether a boat is propelled by oars or motor, and the same boat etiquette must be observed. However, there are some differences in the maneuverability of the power-driven boat.

The following basic rules can normally be used as a foundation for boat handling under power with a right-hand propeller:

1. Boat stopped, rudder right, engine ahead—bow will come right.

2. Boat stopped, rudder left, engine ahead—bow will come left.
3. Boat stopped, rudder any direction, engine astern—bow will come right. Stern will come left. (No wind situation.)
4. Boat moving astern, rudder left, engine stopped—stern will come left.
5. Boat moving astern, rudder right, engine stopped—stern will come right.
6. Boat moving astern, rudder left, engine ahead—bow will come to left.
7. Boat moving astern, rudder right, engine ahead—bow will come to right.
8. Boat moving ahead, rudder amidships, engine astern—stern will come to left or erratic course.

When using a rudder and propeller, the rudder will have no effect when the boat is not moving unless the propeller is in the ahead position causing a wash over the rudder. Boats with a rudder handle very poorly when going astern. The walking effect of the propeller causes a boat with a right-hand propeller to back to port unless this force is overcome by the tendency to back into the wind. If the boat is moving ahead and the engine is shifted astern, a somewhat erratic course may follow. Experience with a specific boat is required before the actual response can be predicted. Even then, the wind and current must be taken into account, because they affect the track of the boat.

Inflatable Life Rafts

In addition to lifeboats, modern ships are provided with inflatable life rafts. These have replaced the older balsa or Carley life rafts and floats. Vessels and tankships that have widely separated accommodations or work areas must have at least one life raft in each such location. Inflatable life rafts have a number of advantages. They are easy to launch; they take up about one-tenth the deck space of a lifeboat of comparable capacity; and, with their proven ability to remain afloat for long periods of time, they provide better survival potential. Disadvantages include limited maneuverability, slow propulsion by paddles, and a propensity to drift because of the boat's lightness.

There are several types of inflatable life rafts on the market, all of which must pass rigid Coast Guard inspection. Depending upon the manufacturer, life rafts have varying characteristics. Some manufacturers provide ladders for boarding. The canopy of one type is rugged enough to permit survivors to jump onto it from the side of the ship. Launching operations also may vary depending upon the particular raft. One example, launching instructions for the RFD Elliott life raft, is shown in figure 19. Because life rafts have different characteristics it is especially important that seamen read carefully the instructions for the life rafts on board their ship before sailing.

The life rafts shown in figures 20 and 21 are typical of those approved by the Coast Guard. The canopy that protects the occupants from cold and dampness is supported by inflatable braces. The towing bridle may be combined with the boarding ladder. The sea anchor, which reduces drift, will keep the head of the raft towards the sea and make it ride more comfortably. The four water pockets fill with water and make the raft more stable. The lifelines on the outside of the raft provide a grip for persons in the water. Similar lifelines on the inside can help the occupants remain in place in severe weather. There is a double floor that can be inflated to help insulate against cold water. A safety knife is provided by the entrance at the end of the raft to cut the painter. The knife cannot cut the fabric of the raft by accident. The raft is designed to catch rainwater to augment the supply of canned water in the raft's original rations. Even so, water should not be issued to occupants for 24 hours. Lights at each end of the canopy operate automatically when the raft is launched.

Figure 22 shows the automatic release of the life raft. In the first drawing it is stowed in its cradle on deck. The operating cord must be attached to the cradle, rail, or some part of the ship's structure as shown in figure 20. Should the ship sink so quickly that there is no time to launch the raft, a hydrostatic release will ensure that the life raft floats free of the

LAUNCHING INSTRUCTIONS

FOR THE

ELLIOT

INFLATABLE LIFE RAFT

CAUTION

SET FOR OPERATION. DO NOT TAMPER. DO NOT DISTURB METAL BANDS.

1. When stowing raft, always connect the steel link to vessel by shackling painter to cradle using ELLIOT WEAK LINK.

2. Before launching the raft by hand, pull out the painter from the container and make it fast to the cleat provided (on the cradle).

3. If necessary to release painter from cradle, break painter Weak Link manually.

4. Release container by pressing knob on the Hydrostatic Release.

5. Launch life raft complete in container.

6. Gather in painter until taut; give strong pull to inflate raft.

Fig. 19. Drawing of RFD Elliot inflatable life raft and launching instructions. Courtesy RFD Elliot Inc.

Fig. 20. An inflatable life raft stowed on deck in cradle.

Fig. 21. This inflatable life raft is found on fishing vessels and yachts. Its unique feature is its large ballast chamber that traps water and stabilizes the raft. This raft has withstood typhoons safely. Its capacity is 6 people. Courtesy Givens Marine Survival Co., Inc.

1

The Elliot life raft is secured to its cradle with a hydrostatic release that, if time permits, can be tripped for manual release and inflation of the raft. If time does not permit manual release and inflation, this is accomplished automatically.

2

As the vessel sinks, pressure of the water at a depth of 10 feet actuates the release mechanism, freeing the raft from its stowage. The life raft is inherently buoyant and will float to the surface.

3

The sinking vessel pulls the operating cord and the life raft inflates. The CO_2 gas expands into the buoyancy chambers in a few seconds so the raft cannot be pulled down by the ship. The sea anchor is streamed automatically when the raft inflates, to reduce drift. All rafts are equipped with a spare sea anchor in the emergency equipment.

4

The Elliot Weak Link attaches the painter to the ship; this parts and permits the raft to float free of the sinking vessel. The water-activated light comes on to guide survivors to the raft. Once aboard, help others to board, and then read the raft manual to learn details of raft operation and other data to ensure survival.

Fig. 22. Automatic release and inflation of life raft. Courtesy RFD Elliot Inc.

cradle at a depth of about 10 feet. The operating cord is attached to the vessel by a "weak link" that will break if the raft is in danger of being dragged down by the sinking vessel. The raft automatically inflates as shown in the third drawing, and is ready to be boarded as shown in the fourth drawing.

Under normal conditions, the life raft is released from the cradle by pressing the knob on the hydrostatic release, carrying it to the rail, and tossing it over the side. The painter is gathered in until taut, and a strong pull on it will start the process of inflating the raft. Although the raft can be inflated on deck, this is not recommended because of the danger of tearing the fabric of the raft when it is manhandled over the side. Should the ship have suffered damage and any sharp edges in holes on the ship's side be present, this could easily happen. Although the raft will float with half its air chambers ruptured and still support its capacity of survivors, there is no point in courting disaster. Life rafts fitted on passenger carrying vessels require davits to launch. The raft may be picked up, swung to the side of the ship, inflated, loaded, and then launched.

Life rafts are provided with an impressive amount of survival equipment: ladder, heaving line, jackknife, lifelines, paddles, sea anchor, towing connections, repair kits, sponges, and bailers. They also contain a survival manual with vital information that should be read by everyone aboard.

Carbon dioxide gas is used to inflate life rafts. Heavy concentrations of this gas can result in unconsciousness leading to death. Therefore, the canopy opening must be adjusted to allow for fresh air. After the raft is inflated, the carbon dioxide exhaled by the survivors will cause some discomfort unless the canopy is kept partially open.

Inflatable life rafts must be inspected by personnel at a certified facility annually. Although rugged, life rafts are designed for one purpose only: to save life. If abused or damaged, they may fail when needed. The fiberglass container is designed to protect the life raft and keep it from the weather. Never tamper with a life raft or any other piece of lifesaving equipment. If a life raft is inflated accidentally, it must be repacked at an approved facility. This is extremely expensive.

Survival Capsules

Some artificial islands and mobile offshore drilling rigs are equipped with survival capsules (fig. 23). The launching mechanism consists of a hold and launch platform, an electric winch, and a single wire rope fall connected to a Rottmer-type hook on top of the capsule. The platform is permanently located so that it extends over the side. Quick launch and recovery operations are possible. Most capsules are equipped with a seawater sprinkling system to provide external fire protection. The capsule is propelled by a diesel engine.

Personal Flotation Devices

In addition to carrying adequate lifeboats and life rafts, all U.S.-flag vessels must carry at least one Coast Guard approved

Fig. 23. Survival capsule. Survival capsules are installed on non-self-propelled drilling rigs, self-propelled drilling rigs, fixed structures, and artificial islands. They vary in capacity from 14 to 50 persons. They are launched at the rate of 2 feet per second by a single fall and can make speeds of up to 6 knots. Courtesy Whittaker Corporation.

PFD (personal flotation device) for each person aboard. These must be inspected annually by the Coast Guard, and those that can no longer pass inspection must be replaced. The Type I PFD is the well-known life jacket that comes in adult and child sizes. The Type I PFD is normally equipped with a light and a whistle.

The Type IV PFD or ring buoy is not intended to be worn, but is thrown to a person in the water. It is held by the person overboard until rescued. When throwing a ring buoy, throw it near, not at, the person.

The Type V PFD (or workvest) is approved for merchant personnel working near or over the water, but it is not a substitute for the Type I and cannot be counted as a Type I at the annual Coast Guard inspection.

In addition to lifeboats and life rafts, ocean passenger vessels must have life floats or buoyant apparatus for emergency use by the passengers. These must be stowed for quick launchings with lashings capable of being easily cast off. Unless skids are provided, buoyant apparatus and life floats must weigh less than 400 pounds to ensure easy launching and are provided with a boat hook, paddles, waterlights, painter, and lifeline.

Immersion Suits

In addition to being able to float, a person in the water must stay warm enough to avoid losing body heat and suffering from the resulting hypothermia. An immersion suit or thermal protective aid is now required for each passenger or crew member on every U.S. flag vessel that operates in cold offshore waters or in harsh and remote regions (fig. 24).

These suits are constructed primarily of closed-cell flexible foam that meets buoyancy and thermal insulation requirements. They must fit properly and form a tight seal around the face. They have light reflective material, and are colored what the Coast Guard calls "vivid reddish green." The wearer's head is maintained above the surface of the water, and the suit must be capable of turning over an unconscious person so that his mouth is clear of the water within

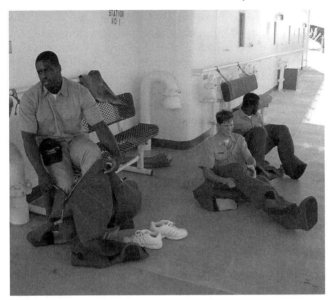

Fig. 24. Immersion suit familiarization aboard T.S. *Golden Bear*.

five seconds. In addition, the wearer must be able to suit up in two minutes. The suit's zipper should be lubricated regularly with paraffin so that it works easily, and the suit should be stowed where it is handy.

Survival suits are both bulky and cumbersome, but they work! You should practice donning your suit before an emergency. Make sure yours fits and is in good condition. The place to put it on is topside, not below decks where it may hamper you in getting to your abandon ship station.

Global Maritime Distress and Safety System (GMDSS)

All large oceangoing vessels are provided with lifeboat radios, which are carried to a lifeboat for drills or when actually abandoning ship. Gone are the bulky lifeboat emergency radios that were hand cranked for power while another person sent an SOS message with a telegraph key. Now, a vessel's GMDSS survival craft equipment includes emergency position indicating radio beacons (EPIRBs), search and rescue transponders (SARTs) and portable very high frequency (VIIF) radios. The EPIRB will signal passing satellites that you are in distress and automatically send your position to rescue centers. As the rescue vessels or aircraft close in on your position, your SART will indicate your exact position on their search radars. Finally, as you hear or see the approaching rescue craft, you can talk to them on your VHF radio to assist in your recovery.

Morse Code

Although manually keyed distress signals in lifeboats are a thing of the past, the author cannot recommend too strongly that anyone who earns his or her living at sea learn the Morse Code. This is only required for licensed deck officers, but in an emergency situation, a seaman who could talk to a rescue ship by flashing light might play a key role in a rescue operation.

For manual keying in the transmission and reception of messages, the Morse Code is given below:

A ·—	J ·———	S ···	2 ··———
B —···	K —·—	T —	3 ···——
C —·—·	L ·—··	U ··—	4 ····—
D —··	M ——	V ···—	5 ·····
E ·	N —·	W ·——	6 —····
F ··—·	O ———	X —··—	7 ——···
G ——·	P ·——·	Y —·——	8 ———··
H ····	Q ——·—	Z ——··	9 ————·
I ··	R ·—·	1 ·————	0 —————

Distress Signals

The following distress signals, contained in Annex IV, 72 COLREGS (International Regulations for Preventing Collision at Sea), are recognized by all maritime nations (figs. 25, 26, and 27).

1. Need of assistance. The following signals, used or exhibited either together or separately, indicate distress and need of assistance:

(a) a gun or other explosive signal fired at intervals of about a minute;

(b) a continuous sounding with any fog-signaling apparatus;

(c) rockets or shells, throwing red stars fired one at a time at short intervals;

(d) a signal made by radiotelegraphy or by any other signaling method consisting of the group . . . — — — . . . (SOS) in the Morse Code;

(e) a signal sent by radiotelephony consisting of the spoken word "Mayday";

(f) the International Code Signal of distress indicated by N.C.;

(g) a signal consisting of a square flag having above or below it a ball or anything resembling a ball;

(h) flames on the vessel (as from a burning tar barrel, oil barrel, etc.);

(i) a rocket parachute flare or a hand flare showing a red light;

(j) a smoke signal giving off orange-colored smoke;

(k) slowly and repeatedly raising and lowering arms outstretched to each side;

(l) the radiotelegraph alarm signal;

(m) the radiotelephone alarm signal;

(n) signals transmitted by emergency position-indicating radio beacons.

2. The use or exhibition of any of the foregoing signals except for the purpose of indicating distress and need of assistance and the use of other signals which may be confused with any of the above signals is prohibited.

3. Attention is drawn to the relevant sections of the International Code of Signals, the *Merchant Ship Search and Rescue Manual,* and the following signals:

(a) a piece of orange-colored canvas with either a black square and circle or other appropriate symbol (for identification from the air);

(b) a dye marker.

I Landing signals for the guidance of small boats with crews or persons in distress

	MANUAL SIGNALS	LIGHT SIGNALS	OTHER SIGNALS	SIGNIFICATION
Day signals	**Vertical** motion of a white flag or of the arms	or firing of a **green** star signal	or code letter **K** given by light or sound-signal apparatus	This is the best place to land
Night signals	**Vertical** motion of a white light or flare	or firing of a **green** star signal	or code letter **K** given by light or sound-signal apparatus	

A range (indication of direction) may be given by placing a steady white light or flare at a lower level and in line with the observer

Day signals	**Horizontal** motion of a white flag or of the arms extended horizontally	or firing of a **red** star signal	or code letter **S** given by light or sound-signal apparatus	Landing here highly dangerous.
Night signals	**Horizontal** motion of a light or flare	or firing of a **red** star signal	or code letter **S** given by light or sound-signal apparatus	

Day signals	1 **Horizontal** motion of a white flag, followed by 2 the placing of the white flag in the ground and 3 by the carrying of another white flag in the direction to be indicated	1 or firing of a **red** star signal vertically and a 2 **white** star signal in the direction towards the better landing place	1 or signalling the code letter **S** (...) followed by the code letter **R** (._.) if a better landing place for the craft in distress is located more to the *right* in the direction of approach 2 or signalling the code letter **S** (...) followed by the code letter **L** (._..) if a better landing place for the craft in distress is located more to the *left* in the direction of approach	Landing here highly dangerous. A more favourable location for landing is in the direction indicated
Night signals	1 **Horizontal** motion of a white light or flare 2 followed by the placing of the white light or flare on the ground and 3 the carrying of another white light or flare in the direction to be indicated	1 or firing of a **red** star signal vertically and a 2 **white** star signal in the direction towards the better landing place	1 or signalling the code letter **S** (...) followed by the code letter **R** (._.) if a better landing place for the craft in distress is located more to the *right* in the direction of approach 2 or signalling the code letter **S** (...) followed by the code letter **L** (._..) if a better landing place for the craft in distress is located more to the *left* in the direction of approach	

II Signals to be employed in connection with the use of shore lifesaving apparatus

	MANUAL SIGNALS	LIGHT SIGNALS	OTHER SIGNALS	SIGNIFICATION
Day signals	**Vertical** motion of a white flag or of the arms	or firing of a **green** star signal		In general: affirmative Specifically: rocket line is held – tail block is made fast – hawser is made fast – man is in the breeches buoy – haul away
Night signals	**Vertical** motion of a white light or flare	or firing of a **green** star signal		

Fig. 25. Table of Lifesaving Signals. Courtesy National Imagery and Mapping Agency from NVPUB102.

Day signals	Horizontal motion of a white flag or of the arms extended horizontally	or firing of a red star signal			In general: negative Specifically: slack away – avast hauling
Night signals	Horizontal motion of a white light or flare	or firing of a red star signal			

III Replies from lifesaving stations or maritime rescue units to distress signals made by a ship or person

Day signals	Orange smoke signal	or combined *light and sound* signal (thunder-light) consisting of 3 single signals which are fired at intervals of approximately one minute		You are seen – assistance will be given as soon as possible (Repetition of such signal shall have the same meaning)
Night signals	White star rocket consisting of 3 single signals which are fired at intervals of approximately one minute			

If necessary, the day signals may be given at night or the night signals by day

IV Signals used by aircraft engaged on search and rescue operations to direct ships towards an aircraft, ship or person in distress

PROCEDURES PERFORMED IN SEQUENCE BY AN AIRCRAFT			SIGNIFICATION
1 Aircraft circles the surface craft at least once	2 Aircraft crosses the surface craft course close ahead at low altitude opening and closing the propeller pitch	3 Aircraft heads in the direction in which the surface craft is to be directed	The aircraft is directing a surface craft towards an aircraft or surface craft in distress (Repetition of such signals shall have the same meaning)
Crossing the surface craft's wake **close astern** at low altitude opening and closing the throttle or changing the propeller pitch			The assistance of the surface craft is no longer required (Repetition of such signals shall have the same meaning)

Fig. 25—*Continued*

Landing on a Beach

Although the lifesaving signals given above provide for communication between the boat crew and beach personnel, landing through heavy surf is highly dangerous and should not be attempted. Lifeboats are not surfboats. Beamy lifeboats or rafts handle poorly in the surf and will easily broach or capsize. Survivors in lifeboats are well advised to wait for rescue by helicopter or other rescue craft. Beach landings should be attempted only in an extreme emergency. However, if beaching through surf is absolutely necessary to save

Fig. 26. Storm warning signals. Whenever winds dangerous to navigation are forecast for an area, the signals shown above may be hoisted. The signals indicate that the mariner can expect these weather conditions within the next 12 hours.

life or limb, the following procedures are generally recommended:

1. Boats under oars should be landed with the bow to the sea. Remember that surf always looks less severe from seaward. This allows better control by the coxswain using his sweep oar to assist in keeping the bow to the sea. A sea anchor can be used from the bow to assist in con-

Fig. 27. Manual distress signal for daytime use. The signal illustrated in the drawing is made by slowly and repeatedly raising and lowering the arms outstretched to each side. This signal is simple, needing no special equipment. The visibility of the signal is improved by holding in each hand a handkerchief, towel, bathing suit, or other attention-getting material.

trolling the boat. In between swells, back water to move the boat closer to the beach. *Do not rush this operation.* Disembark all hands immediately when the boat lands.

2. Power boats or flemming gear propelled boats may normally be landed best by using the available oars and landing in the same way as a boat under oars. However, this requires persons who are physically fit and well trained.

3. If a power boat must be landed under propeller power, a bow first landing is usually the only feasible way. A sea anchor should be towed astern to assist maneuvering. Landing a power boat is *not* recommended under any circumstances.

4. Life rafts have minimum control, so beaching through surf is extremely hazardous and should be avoided. If beaching becomes inevitable or is required in an emergency, take advantage of wind and sea. Avoid rocky areas if possible and keep all weight low in the raft to avoid capsizing. All hands should disembark as soon as the

raft grounds, and the raft should be pulled up to the high
water mark.

Rescue of a Person Overboard and Survivors in the Water

At the first cry of "man overboard," a ring buoy should be
thrown to mark the spot and to give the person something
with which to keep afloat if possible. The rudder should be
turned in the direction of the person to prevent the propeller
from striking him. In the daytime a smoke distress signal
will help mark the position of the victim overboard, whereas
at night a flare or water light attached to the ring buoy will
serve the same purpose.

At all cost, the person overboard should be kept in sight.
Someone on board should be directed to do this and perform
no other duty. If the person can be kept in sight, a circle recovery maneuver is the quickest way to bring the victim back
aboard in daytime. Recovery of a person by ship or by lifeboat
will depend upon the weather and other factors.

At night the Williamson turn is the best means of bring-
ing the overboard victim aboard even though it takes somewhat longer than a circle recovery (fig. 28). To execute the

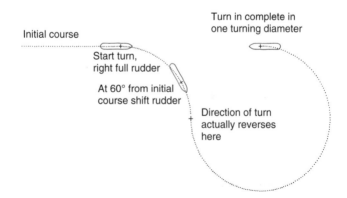

Fig. 28. The Williamson turn.

Williamson turn, the rudder is put over hard towards the side from which the person has fallen overboard. The rudder is continued full until the ship is 60° from the original heading, and then shifted full to the opposite direction. The ship continues to turn in the new direction until steadied up on the opposite (or reciprocal) of the original course. When the ship is on the reciprocal course, the victim should be close aboard the bow on the side from which he or she fell.

The approach to a person who is to be picked up in the water is much like the approach to a landing with the added factor that the victim will drift to leeward with the wind and sea while a dock or pier will not.

The parent ship should be to windward of and as close as possible to the victim when the boat is put in the water, in order to reduce the time the victim will have to spend in the boat, as well as to shorten the trip the boat will make to pick up the individual in the open ocean.

The most important factor is the safety of the boat, because a swamped boat will be of no use to the individual in the water. With the ship to weather of the rescue boat and the victim, the boat should approach the victim as directly as possible to save time and avoid missing the approach. In the bow of the boat, the crew members should be ready to pass a ring buoy, line, or boat hook to the victim, or to dive in with a line and ring buoy to assist in pulling the victim on board the boat. Voice radio contact should be maintained between the ship and the boat in order that the ship can be prepared to receive the victim on the return of the boat.

Helicopter Evacuation

Helicopter evacuation for merchant ship personnel requiring urgent medical assistance is available in many areas of the world. This is a hazardous undertaking on the part of the helicopter pilot and crew and requires both cooperation and good seamanship on the part of the merchant ship. The Coast Guard requires that instructions for this maneuver be posted in the pilothouse of all vessels. Read them! Some of the most important points are:

1. Do *not* shine any lights on the helicopter at night.
2. Have the hoist area clear of obstructions. The area should have at least a 50-foot radius.
3. The patient should be as close to the hoist area as possible and ready for transfer.
4. The basket or stretcher should touch the deck prior to handling to avoid shock.
5. Do *not* secure the cable from the helicopter to the vessel.
6. The master should choose the course so that wind is on the bow and stack gases are clear of the hoist area.

Sample Multiple-Choice Questions for Lifeboatman Examination

The lifeboatman examination given by the Coast Guard consists of a written and a practical test. The written test poses 70 multiple-choice questions. The sample that follows has been taken from published banks of questions which the Coast Guard uses in preparing questions for use in the examining room. The prospective lifeboatman is cautioned that sometimes a few able seaman questions may turn up on the lifeboatman exam. Similarly, lifeboatman questions may turn up on the able seaman exam. So the wise applicant will not try to "get by" by studying as little as possible. Simply knowing the answers to the questions given here won't do. The letter of the correct answer to each question is set in boldface type.

1. The way to operate the hand-held distress flare is to:
   a. remove cap and pull ignitor wire
   b. remove cap and scratch handle on hard object
   c. remove cap and scratch button on flare against the surface on the cap
   d. turn cap clockwise

2. Who should test and inspect an inflatable life raft?
   a. Chief Mate
   b. qualified sales and service representative

c. shipyard personnel
d. certified lifeboatman

3. Inflatable life rafts are provided with:
   a. a Very pistol
   b. a towing connection
   c. a portable radio
   d. canned milk

4. Life rafts must be overhauled and inspected at least every:
   a. 6 months
   b. 12 months
   c. 18 months
   d. 24 months

5. The purpose of underwater pockets on a life raft is to:
   a. store rain water
   b. stabilize the raft
   c. stow life raft equipment
   d. aid in righting the raft if it inflates upside down

6. Where is the knife in a life raft located?
   a. in the first aid kit
   b. on a line hanging down from the canopy
   c. in the equipment bag
   d. in a pocket on the edge of the raft

7. The primary purpose of the hydrostatic release on a life raft is to:
   a. inflate the life raft
   b. test the pressure in the raft
   c. hold raft on its cradle
   d. release the raft if the vessel sinks

8. How do you hand launch a life raft?
   a. pull a cord
   b. cut metal restraining bands
   c. remove elastic packing strap
   d. throw the container overboard

9. The best way to release a life raft from its cradle is by:
   a. cutting the metal straps
   b. the screw turnbuckle on the back of the cradle
   c. lifting one end of the raft
   d. pushing the plunger on the center of the hydrostatic release

10. A life raft should be manually released from its cradle by:
    a. cutting the straps
    b. Rottmer Release
    c. Static release
    d. Hydrostatic release-pushing plunger

11. What position should a person assume if in the sea wearing a life jacket for an extended period of time?
    a. assume spar position; legs extended down, arms spread
    b. legs and arms spread apart lying on back
    c. knees tucked up to chin
    d. lying on stomach face underwater except for breathing

12. A ship's abandon ship signal is:
    a. 6 short blasts and 1 long blast
    b. 1 long for 10 seconds
    c. more than 6 short blasts and 1 long blast
    d. 6 short blasts, more than 1 long blast

13. The lights on the outside of the canopy of an inflatable life raft operate:
    a. by turning on a switch located inside the canopy
    b. only at night
    c. light sensor
    d. automatically

14. When lowering the life raft by hand, what operation should take place?
    a. operating cord detaches automatically
    b. operating cord should be attached to some substantial part of the ship

   c. you should open casing by cutting metal straps
   d. you should inflate the raft on deck first

15. Which operation should be done when launching a portable life raft?
   a. open red valve on CO_2 apparatus
   b. secure operating cord to the vessel
   c. after inflation, detach operation cord from life raft
   d. open life raft casing

16. When a life raft is launched, the operating cord is used for:
   a. a sea painter
   b. cut out and thrown away
   c. to secure the boarding ladder
   d. an emergency fishing line

17. When in a life raft in very cold weather, the greatest danger is:
   a. sharks
   b. freezing
   c. danger of CO_2 from keeping canopy closed
   d. starvation

18. The inflatable bottom on the life raft is to protect you from cold and:
   a. CO_2 asphyxiation
   b. warm water
   c. rough water
   d. to keep the sides of the raft full of air

19. The purpose of oil in the sea anchor is:
   a. to weigh down the anchor
   b. to lubricate the anchor
   c. to repel dangerous fish
   d. to help smooth the sea

20. The operating cord of an inflatable life raft is also used as:
   a. tow line

   b. painter
   c. orange smoke flares
   d. lifeline

21. When reaching ashore in a life raft, the *first* thing to do is:
   a. secure the life raft for possible use as a shelter
   b. go get some firewood
   c. remove the provisions from the life raft
   d. abandon the life raft and send it out to sea in hopes that someone will spot it

22. Signaling device provided in the inflatable life raft is:
   a. Very pistol
   b. orange smoke flares
   c. air horn
   d. lantern

23. The floor of the life raft can be inflated by:
   a. launching raft overboard pull cord
   b. hand pump in tool bag
   c. extra CO_2 canisters for floor
   d. bleeding air out of the sides

24. To haul a life raft back on board, you should:
   a. hook line to eye on raft
   b. pass lines under the raft
   c. hook line to towing bridles
   d. deflate the raft

25. When using the handheld type signaling mirror, one hand is used to hold the mirror and the other:
   a. is held behind the mirror
   b. is held in front of the mirror
   c. used to shield the eyes
   d. used to shield the mirror

26. When lowering boat during rough weather it is advisable to:

a. avoid the use of frapping lines as it may endanger the boat

b. lower the boat near the water and have crew board using embarkation ladder

c. release tricing pendant before removing boat from cradle

d. have heaving line ready and standing by

27. You are in a raft, drifting at sea, which of the following is an indication of land nearby?
    a. fog
    b. cumulus clouds
    c. birds
    d. flying fish

28. The tricing pendant should be released:
    a. before the boat is lowered
    b. before the passengers get in
    c. after the passengers get in
    d. after the boat is afloat

29. If you are headed 270° True in a life raft, you are going:
    a. north
    b. south
    c. east
    d. west

30. Life rafts are less maneuverable than lifeboats due to their weight, shallow draft and:
    a. large number of appurtenances
    b. large sail area
    c. greater amount of equipment
    d. inability to withstand heavy seas

31. If the inflatable life raft is to be taken in tow, the towline is to be connected to the:
    a. towing connection (bridle)
    b. life line

    c. boarding ladder
    d. all of the above

32. Which of the following would help to survive an extended period in a life raft?
    a. wet clothing to prevent the body from dehydration
    b. keep the raft pumped up as hard as possible
    c. keep busy
    d. all of the above

33. The error in a magnetic compass caused by the vessel's magnetism is called:
    a. variation
    b. deviation
    c. compass error
    d. bearing error

34. The lever for the mechanical disengaging apparatus on a lifeboat shall be marked by:
    a. painting the lever white
    b. painting the area around the lever red
    c. the words "Danger Lever Lowers Boat"
    d. painting the lever red

35. Water should not be issued to occupants (healthy people) of a life raft for:
    a. 8 hours
    b. 10 hours
    c. 24 hours
    d. 48 hours

36. BOTH INTERNATIONAL AND INLAND Which signal, other than a distress signal, can be used by a vessel to attract attention?
    a. searchlight beam
    b. continuous sounding of a fog signal apparatus
    c. burning barrel
    d. orange smoke signal

37. The command, in a boat under oars, to complete the stroke and place oars in the boat:
    a. oars
    b. way enough
    c. hold water
    d. in bows

38. When a sea anchor is used in landing in a heavy surf, headway is checked by:
    a. slacking the tripping line and towing the apex end forward
    b. slacking the tripping line and towing the mouth forward by the holding line
    c. towing with the tripping line and the holding line slack
    d. towing the apex end forward with the tripping line

39. The floating orange smoke signal is ignited:
    a. automatically by water
    b. by a small pull wire
    c. by striking the cap on the striker bottom
    d. by lighting a match

40. If you must swim through an oil fire, you should NOT:
    a. wear as much clothing as possible
    b. enter the water feet first
    c. swim with the wind
    d. cover eyes with one hand when entering the water

41. The purpose of air tanks in a lifeboat is to:
    a. help the lifeboat float
    b. add strength to the lifeboat
    c. keep lifeboat afloat if boat becomes flooded
    d. put in provisions

42. When first using the compass in a lifeboat you must be careful to:
    a. be sure to mount it on the centerline of the boat

    b. add western variation to error

    c. disregard deviation because the lifeboat is so small compared to the ship

    d. check compass for error at noon

43. An immersion suit must be equipped with a(n):
    a. air bottle for breathing
    b. whistle and light
    c. whistle, light, and reflective tape
    d. whistle, light, and sea dye marker

44. Most enclosed lifeboats will right themselves after capsizing IF the:
    a. lowest ballast tanks are filled with water
    b. fuel tanks are not less than half full
    c. passengers are strapped to their seats
    d. sea anchor is deployed to windward

45. Which primarily functions as a support?
    a. limber hole
    b. thwart
    c. stanchion
    d. footing

46. What is the length of the heaving line on an inflatable life raft?
    a. 10 meters
    b. 20 meters
    c. 30 meters
    d. 40 meters

47. The greatest hazard to survival of a person in the sea is:
    a. weakening of the muscles due to wave action
    b. muscle cramps
    c. exposure to sun and wind
    d. loss of body heat

48. The most commonly used davit on merchant vessels today is:

    a. radial
    b. sheath screw
    c. gravity
    d. quadrantal

49. Limit switches must be tested at least once every:
    a. week
    b. month
    c. 2 months
    d. 3 months

50. The grab rail of a metal lifeboat is normally located:
    a. along the turn of the bilge
    b. along each side of the keel
    c. near the top of the gunwale
    d. at the bow and at the stern

51. What is the most important thing to check before lowering a boat?
    a. oars
    b. life jackets
    c. sea painter
    d. boat plug

52. One short blast of the whistle means:
    a. secure lifeboats
    b. raise boats
    c. lower boats
    d. drill is over

53. When lowering a lifeboat to the embarkation deck, which of the following are used to bring the boat to the side of the ship?
    a. pull lines
    b. boat hooks
    c. tricing pendants
    d. frapping line

54. The canopy of an inflatable life raft should:
    a. go into place as the raft is inflated

b. be put up after everyone is aboard
c. be put up only in severe weather
d. be used as a sail if the wind is blowing

55. When operating the air supply system in a covered life-boat, the:
   a. fuel supply valve should be closed
   b. hatches, doors, and oar ports should be closed
   c. air cylinder shut-off valve should be closed
   d. engine should be shut off

56. The boat command meaning "complete the stroke, stop rowing, and hold blades flat" is:
   a. "Oars"
   b. "Up oars"
   c. "Way enough"
   d. "Hold water"

57. After launching an inflatable raft should be kept dry inside by:
   a. opening the automatic drain plugs
   b. draining the water pockets
   c. using the electric bilge pump
   d. using the bailers and cellulose sponge

58. Lines passed around the falls to hold the boat while passengers are boarding are:
   a. life lines
   b. frapping lines
   c. tricing lines
   d. tripping lines

59. Inflatable liferafts are provided with a:
   a. jackknife
   b. towing connection
   c. lifeline
   d. all of the above

60. If the coxswain of your lifeboat gives the command "Hold Water" you should:
    a. complete the stroke, raise your oar slightly, swinging the oar slightly forward, and place it in the boat
    b. lift the oar into a vertical position
    c. used to enable oarsmen to rest their arms after a long row
    d. dip the blade of your oar into the water vertically and hold it perpendicular to the keel line

61. Inflatable liferafts are provided with:
    a. portable radio
    b. oil lantern
    c. canned milk
    d. towing bridle

62. The purpose of the wire stretched between the davit heads is to:
    a. keep the movements of the davits at the same speed
    b. keep the davits from slipping when they are in the stowed position
    c. prevent vibration during lowering of the boat
    d. support the man-ropes

63. The falls on gravity davits are:
    a. manila
    b. nylon
    c. wire
    d. any of the above

64. A person has fallen overboard and is being picked up with a lifeboat. If the person appears in danger of drowning, the lifeboat should be maneuvered to make:
    a. an approach from leeward
    b. a direct approach
    c. the most direct approach
    d. an approach from across wind

65. When a man who has fallen overboard is being picked up by a lifeboat, the boat should approach with the wind:
    a. astern and the victim just off the bow
    b. ahead and the victim just off the bow
    c. just off the bow and the victim to windward
    d. just off the bow and the victim to leeward

66. When evacuating a seaman by helicopter lift, the vessel should be:
    a. stopped with the wind dead ahead
    b. stopped with the wind on the beam
    c. underway with the wind 30 degrees on the bow
    d. underway on a course to provide no apparent wind

67. You have abandoned ship and find yourself aboard a lifeboat in a heavy sea. Your boat is able to make way through the water. To prevent broaching you should:
    a. put the sea on your stern and run as fast as the boat will go
    b. take no action to prevent broaching as this is recommended maneuver in a heavy sea
    c. head boat into swells to take them at a 30 to 40 degree angle on either bow, run as slow as possible without losing steerage
    d. place everyone as far forward as possible to keep the boat "bow heavy"

68. Which of the following davit types may be operated by one man?
    a. quadrantal
    b. gravity
    c. sheath-screw
    d. radial

69. Where should the station bills be posted?
    a. crew's quarters area
    b. dining area
    c. vessel control room
    d. all of the above

70. Fire and abandon ship stations and duties may be found on the:
    a. crewman's duty list
    b. certificate of inspection
    c. shipping articles
    d. station bill

71. In rough weather, when a ship is able to maneuver, it is best to launch a lifeboat:
    a. on the lee side
    b. on the windward side
    c. with the wind ahead
    d. with the wind from astern

72. When a ship is abandoned and there are several rafts in the water, one of the first things to be done is:
    a. separate the rafts as much as possible to increase chances of detection
    b. transfer all supplies to one raft
    c. transfer all the injured to one raft
    d. secure the rafts together to keep them from drifting apart

73. While at your lifeboat station, you hear a signal consisting of two short blasts of the whistle. This indicates:
    a. abandon ship
    b. commence lowering boats
    c. stop lowering boats
    d. secure from boat stations

74. Which of the following is *not* required by law to be posted aboard a vessel?
    a. Certificate of Inspection
    b. Official Crew List
    c. officer's licenses
    d. Station Bill

75. What is meant by the term "two blocked?"
    a. The bottom block touches the top block.

    b. The line has jumped the sheaves.
    c. There are turns in the fall.
    d. You have two blocks.

76. A "bowline" is used to:
    a. join lines of equal size
    b. form a temporary eye (loop) in the end of a line
    c. be a stopper
    d. keep a line from fraying

77. When evacuating a seaman by helicopter lift, which of the following statements is true?
    a. The vessel should be stopped with the wind dead ahead during the hoisting operation.
    b. Flags should be flown to provide a visual reference as to the direction of the apparent wind.
    c. The drop line should be grounded first then secured as close to the hoist point as possible.
    d. The hoist area should be located as far aft as possible so the pilot will have a visual reference while approaching.

78. Safety equipment on board vessels must be approved by the:
    a. Coast Guard
    b. Safety Standards Bureau
    c. Occupational Health & Safety Agency (OSHA)
    d. National Safety Council

79. While underway in thick fog you are on watch and hear the cry "Man Overboard." What would you expect the watch officer to do?
    a. Be sure the man is clear, back down until stopped, then send a boat
    b. round turn
    c. race track turn
    d. Williamson turn

80. Which of the following statements about the William-son turn is false?
   a. It requires the highest degree of shiphandling skills to accomplish.
   b. It is the slowest of methods used in turning the vessel.
   c. It is the best turn to use when the victim is not in sight due to reduced visibility.
   d. It returns the vessel to the original trackline on a reciprocal course.

81. When a sea anchor for a lifeboat is properly rigged, it will do which of the following?
   a. Prevent the lifeboat from drifting.
   b. Help to prevent broaching
   c. Prevent the lifeboat from pitching.
   d. None of the above.

82. What word is an international distress signal when sent by radiotelephone?
   a. Securité
   b. Mayday
   c. Breaker
   d. Pan

83. The master shall insure that each deck from which life-boats are launched is:
   a. surfaced with a nonskid texture
   b. roped off to prevent unnecessary access
   c. kept clear of any obstructions that would interfere with launching
   d. posted with a list of persons assigned to the lifeboat

84. When may a work vest be substituted for a required life preserver?
   a. To replace a damaged life preserver
   b. For use during fire drills
   c. For use during boat drills
   d. At no time

85. What does "EPIRB" stand for?
    a. Emergency Position Indicating Radar Buoy
    b. Electronic Pulse Indicating Radiobeacon
    c. Emergency Position Indicating Radiobeacon
    d. None of the above

86. Preparation of Station Bills and signing of same is the responsibility of the:
    a. chief officer of the vessel
    b. owner of the vessel
    c. master of the vessel
    d. United States Coast Guard

87. Which statement is TRUE concerning lifesaving equipment?
    a. The master may assign an officer to keep the lifesaving equipment in good condition.
    b. All lifeboat winch control apparatuses are required to be examined every month.
    c. Nothing may be stowed in a lifeboat other than the required equipment.
    d. All of the above.

88. A placard containing instructions for use of the breeches buoy (Form CG-811) shall be placed:
    a. in the pilothouse and engine room
    b. in the messroom(s)
    c. where available to the watch officer
    d. where best visible in the officer's and crew's quarters

2. Fire

All seamen must be conscious of the danger of fire and should continuously update their knowledge and skills in fire prevention, fire detection, and firefighting. The risk of fire at sea is always present, and the results of fire are too often tragic. A study of the fires aboard the *Morro Castle, Lakonia,* and *Prinsendam* is very sobering and educational. The brief treatment of fire in this book sketches only those aspects pertaining to control and extinguishment as well as fighting various kinds of fire. For those who wish a more complete study, the reader is directed to the International Fire Service Training Association publication, "Marine Fire Fighting." The publication is available from the Oklahoma State University, Fire Protection Publications, 930 North Willis, Stillwater, Oklahoma, 74078.

Elements of Fire and Its Control

Although fire is a complex phenomenon, it consists basically of four parts or components, which are fuel, heat, oxygen, and a chain reaction, as shown in figure 29. The control and extinguishment of ordinary fires in general is brought about by eliminating any one of the components. If oxygen (air) can be diluted or smothered out, the flame will go out. If heat can be taken away by cooling the fuel to a temperature below that at which it will take fire, then the fire can no longer exist. If the chain reaction can be interrupted, flame and heat cannot be formed; therefore, there will be no fire. For the purposes of this manual, it is assumed aboard ship that, except in rare cases, it will be impossible to remove the

Fig. 29. Elements of fire—the fire tetrahedron. Although sometimes described as the "fire triangle," the term "fire tetrahedron," or four-sided figure, is a better explanation of the nature of fire. Fuel, heat, and oxygen can be considered the sides of the figure, and the base is the chain reaction or combustion. If any one of the sides of the figure is lacking, the tetrahedron will not be complete and will fall apart. There will be no chain reaction.

fuel from the heat and the oxygen in order to put the fire out. Therefore, the task of the firefighter will be to reduce the temperature (to cool the fire), to isolate the fire from its supply of oxygen (to smother the fire), or to interrupt the chain reaction, and to accomplish these with the greatest possible speed.

Transmission of heat. Heat may be transmitted in three ways: by radiation, by conduction, and by convection. Through radiation heat is transmitted in direct rays, equally in all directions. Decks and bulkheads are heated by radiation. The heat passes through them by conduction to ignite combustibles on the opposite side, either directly by conduction or by radiation and convection.

Conduction is the process in which the molecules of a substance are heated by molecules having a higher temperature with which they are in contact. The rate of heat transfer by conduction varies with the substance. Some substances conduct heat more readily than others. Steel bulkheads are excellent conductors, and will remain unaffected while transmitting heat to dangerous combustibles.

In convection, portions of gases and liquids that are heated to a higher temperature than the rest of their mass become lighter in weight and move upward into the cooler portions above. It is by convection that heated air and other heated gases rise over a fire and are carried by the wind to ignite combustibles at some distance away. This process is particularly applicable to ventilation systems aboard ships, which may carry the heated gases to places far removed from the fire.

Removal of fuel. When dealing with the removal of the fuel, the firefighter on board ship must take whatever measures possible to prevent additional fuel from coming into contact with the fire since he cannot, in most cases, entirely separate the combustibles from the fire. Firefighters must be ready at all times to shift combustibles to safe areas. Jettisoning deck cargo in danger of catching fire and shutting off valves to stop the flow of liquid fuel to a fire are elementary precautions.

Removal of heat. Another method of extinguishing fire is to deal with the second component—heat. Normally, the best way to remove heat is by the use of water and water sprays and by ventilating to outside areas, except in a compartment where it is possible to close off openings and thus smother the fire.

Removal or control of air (oxygen). The third component of fire—air—is difficult to control. Usually it is practically impossible to remove air from the atmosphere surrounding the fire. However, it can be diluted with other gases which are noncombustible, such as CO_2 (carbon dioxide), or excluded (smothered) with foam, so that extinguishment of the fire will occur.

Removing the supply of oxygen and cooling the blazing substance below those temperatures where fire occurs are the most useful methods of stopping fire. In cargo holds, oxygen is kept out by closing all openings to the atmosphere. Ventilation is stopped, hatches and manholes battened down, and oxygen present is displaced or diluted with CO_2 or steam.

Most modern ships are fitted with CO_2 extinguishing systems. CO_2 is a gas that will not ordinarily support combustion. It will not support human life. Engine rooms fitted with CO_2 extinguishing systems have alarm bells caused to ring by the gas as it is released. When these bells sound, all personnel in the space should get out. In holds or other spaces, men should be warned to get out before CO_2 is released.

Because CO_2 is an inert gas, it does not readily react with materials to change their properties. CO_2 does not damage cargo in a hold, as steam or water might. Aside from its hazard to personnel, its principal drawback is that only a limited quantity is available aboard ship. This requires that the space afire be kept closed off and the gas be used carefully. Vessels fitted with CO_2 systems usually have a chart on the bridge and in the CO_2 room. These set forth the number of bottles to release in order to inert the atmosphere of any specific area of the ship against fire.

Because the gas in the CO_2 bottles is kept under a pressure of up to 2000 pounds per square inch, such bottles should be handled with care and their temperature kept below 130° Fahrenheit. CO_2 is heavier than air and is the familiar "dry ice" in its solid form. In the open air, dry ice goes directly to a gas, but under the high pressure in the cylinder it exists as a liquid. When released, it forms particles of dry ice from the cooling effect of expansion. Human skin can be "burned" by the intense cold as this gas is released from under pressure.

In older ships a steam-smothering system may be installed in the engineering spaces. If installed, steam is used in much the same manner as CO_2. Because of condensation more steam is required than CO_2, and it has been found to be less effective. For this reason, it is no longer approved for installation in newly constructed American-flag vessels.

Controlling chain reactions. Although the actions of certain extinguishing dusts, powders, or finely divided dry chemicals are not fully understood, sufficient work has been done to indicate that the vapors from burning substances progress through a chain of chemical reactions. Therefore, the introduction of an inhibiting powder is able to break the progress from link to link of the chain so that the chemical reactions that result in the fire stop. A commonly used chemical inhibitor has been Halon, but it is being phased out because of environmental considerations. No new installations are being authorized, but existing ones can be utilized.

Halon can be used for:

Class A fires if not deep seated
Class B fires
Class C fires
Fires in storage areas where articles of high value may be
    damaged by residue from other agents.

Ignition temperature. The ignition temperature of a substance is the lowest temperature at which its vapor, usually a gas generated through the application of heat, will ignite independently of any external source of ignition. A substance or its vapor, however, does not have to be heated to its ignition temperature throughout in order for it to be ignited with an external source of ignition.

Petroleum oils ignite, without any external source of ignition, at 490°F to 765°F, which is several hundred degrees higher than their "flash points"; butter and cooking greases ignite at 650°F to 750°F and "flash" at lower temperatures; wood ignites at 450° to 520°F. Each substance has different "fire" and "flash points," neither of which has any relationship to the other. The firefighter, fortunately, does not have to memorize these temperatures, but a general knowledge of them serves as a constant reminder that combustibles in the vicinity of a fire have, in comparison with the heat of the fire, relatively low "ignition temperatures" and that, as a consequence, there is an ever-present danger that fire will spread to them.

Fire point. The fire point is the lowest temperature at which a substance will give off vapors, which, when ignited, will continue to burn. The fire point is generally slightly above the flash point.

Flash point. The flash point is the lowest temperature at which a substance will give off enough vapors to form flammable mixtures of vapors and air (oxygen) immediately above its surface. The temperature at which this mixture will "flash" across the surface (but not burn), if a source of ignition is applied, is the flash point.

In the case of the flash point, the temperature is not high enough to increase the rate of "vaporization" to the point where it will generate a constant supply of fuel.

Vaporization. The rate of vaporization depends on the vapor pressure, which increases with the temperature. A flammable substance is, therefore, more hazardous at an elevated temperature than at normal temperature. It is pointed out that the solid or liquid substances do not burn; only the vapor, which has combined with the oxygen in the air burns. The oxygen must be present to unite with the vapor in flame. Without oxygen the flame will smother.

The tendency of a liquid to vaporize is indicated by its flash point and fire point. The heat of a fire once started naturally increases the temperature of the liquid up to its boiling point. At this point the fire may no longer increase greatly in intensity because the heat supplied to the liquid by radiation from the fire approaches a maximum value, which is balanced by the heat used up in vaporizing or boiling the liquid. When a liquid is burning, its exposed surface is at, or above, the temperature corresponding to its fire point. If the burning liquid can be cooled below this temperature, the rate of vaporization will not provide sufficient fuel (vapor) to support continuous combustion.

Spontaneous ignition or combustion. When heat is generated by chemical action within a substance and the process continues to a point of ignition, the phenomenon is known as spontaneous ignition or spontaneous combustion. Usually, spontaneous heating begins with a slow oxidation that generates heat. As the heat increases the chemical action takes place at a progressively increasing rate until the "ignition temperature" is reached. Some substances reach the ignition temperature rapidly; other substances may take hours or days or even months; while other substances are not subject to spontaneous combustion. Substances subject to spontaneous combustion will differ in the degree of probability with which it will occur, but every such substance has a point in the scale of temperatures at which it will begin to burn. Oils that combine readily with the oxygen in the air are subject to spontaneous heating. When these oils (chiefly of animal or vegetable origin) are present in waste, rubbish, or other material, under conditions in which heat is produced faster than it is dissipated, the temperature rises and ignition may occur.

Explosive range. The temperature at which a flammable substance begins to burn is not necessarily the point at which it will explode. Although heat is a factor in causing explosions, the concentration of certain explosive gases in air within a container or enclosure is a determining cause of the explosion. In the case of gasoline, a vapor-air (oxygen) mixture containing more than 6 percent vapor is too "rich" to explode, and a mixture of less than 1.4 percent is too "lean" to explode. The range from 1.4 to 6 percent is the explosive range for gasoline. Concentrations below or above this range are said to be either "too lean" or "too rich" to explode. The concentration varies among explosive gases and it varies for the same gas under different conditions.

Classifying types of fires. Fire may be classified into four groups. These types are as follows:

Class A—Fires in ordinary combustible materials, such as mattresses, dunnage, piles of wood and shaving, canvas, etc. These fires are best extinguished by the quenching and cooling effects of quantities of water or water fog.

Class B—Fires in substances such as gasoline, oil, lubricating oil, diesel oil, tar, greases, etc. Here the blanketing or smothering effect of the extinguishing agent is of primary importance.

Class C—Fires in live electrical equipment, such as switchboard insulation, transformer terminals, etc. Here the extinguishing agents must be nonconducting so that electrical shock is not experienced by the firefighter.

Class D—Fires in combustible metals such as magnesium, sodium, titanium, lithium, etc. Here, extinguishers require specialized, specific extinguishing agents (fig. 30).

Fig. 30. Classes of fire.

Fighting a Fire

Fighting a fire is a subject that could fill several dozen volumes the size of this small book. Suffice it to say that the sailor's best approach to a fire on board ship is to prevent it from happening in the first place. If this fails, then early discovery and quick and correct extinguishing is the best method of preserving the vessel.

Prevention. Prevention of fire is best accomplished by three actions. The first is to train the crew properly in the normal practice of good seamanship to avoid permitting the fire to take place. Examples of fire prevention behavior are

1. Don't smoke in bed.
2. Don't throw cigarettes in wastebaskets.
3. Don't overload or jury-rig electrical circuits.
4. Dispose of oily rags correctly.

The second important factor in preventing fire is proper maintenance. Frequent inspection of wiring and regular inspection and cleaning of galley exhaust vents is important.

Smoke detection systems should be inspected and checked regularly.

The third and most important factor is proper training and planning for a fire. This may prevent a minor smoldering cord or small trash can fire from engulfing the entire ship.

Should a fire be discovered, see that it is reported to the proper authority at once. *After* the fire has been reported, take action to contain or control the fire until the ship's organization is brought into play.

It is important that crew members use common sense in the initial attack on a fire. If the fire is in an enclosed space, be sure you have a safe and unblockable means of escape and an alternate escape route. Be aware that smoke inhalation and reduced oxygen may cause loss of consciousness.

Finally, you must choose the correct extinguishing agent. If electricity is involved, soda acid or salt water must *never* be used. If it is a burning mattress or lumber, CO_2 is not very effective.

During preliminary attacks on fire, primary importance must be placed on individual safety. More detailed firefighting techniques are available in other texts. Remember, you can never learn too much about fire. Your life and your ship's survival are on the line.

Portable fire extinguishers. Listed below are three types of portable extinguishers commonly used on merchant vessels, the type of fires for which they are suitable, the method of operation, and the maintenance required:

Foam

Use on: Class A and Class B fires. Do not use on electrical fires.

How to operate: Turn upside down. Direct nozzle at base of fire. Recharge.

Yearly maintenance: Discharge. Clean hose and inside of extinguisher thoroughly. Recharge as directed on nameplate.

Carbon Dioxide

Use on: Class B and Class C fires. CO_2 extinguishers are not permitted in passenger or crew quarters.

How to operate: Open valve to release snow and gas. Direct discharge at flames in a slow sweeping motion.

Yearly maintenance: Weigh. Recharge if weight is 10 percent or more under required charge. Check hose and horn.

Dry Chemical

Use on: Class B and Class C fires (fig. 31).

How to operate: Operate release and direct discharge at base of flames in sweeping motion.

Yearly maintenance: Examine pressure cartridge and replace if end is punctured or if the cartridge has leaked. See that dry chemical is not caked. In pressure type, see that pressure gauge is in operating range and that there is sufficient quantity of dry chemical.

Special purpose extinguisher: Special purpose extinguishers are available for some of the class D type fires and are carried when these materials are present. Many of these class D materials do not have portable type fire extinguishing and the only solution to a fire is to isolate and let the fire burn itself out.

Fig. 31. (A) A foam fire extinguisher. (B) A carbon dioxide extinguisher. (C) A dry chemical extinguisher.

Firefighting techniques. Fire in explosives and certain other dangerous substances, such as ammonium nitrate (NH_4NO_3), cannot always be put out by using CO_2 or steam. Many such substances can provide their own oxygen. These fires can often be fought with water. Powdered magnesium metal can burn in CO_2. Sodium metal will burn vigorously in water. When these types of cargo are carried, careful consideration should be given to shipper's instructions, pertinent dangerous cargo regulations, and other responsible sources of information, so that proper action will be known in event of fire.

An efficient method of fighting oil fires is the use of water spray applied with a combination nozzle. Spray nozzles disperse the water in the form of fine droplets. This increases the speed with which the cooling capacity of the water becomes effective, reducing the amount of water required to cool a fire below the temperature at which burning will occur. In addition to putting out fires on the surface of liquids, an important use of fog may be the cooling of bulkheads of a compartment enclosing a fire. Fog also can be used as a shield behind which it is possible to advance in putting out a fire. Temperatures must be lowered beneath the point at which reignition will occur behind you as you advance using the fog nozzle (fig. 32). Care must be taken that sufficient oxygen is present to sustain life after a fire that used oxygen within a space. Fixed water spray systems are also used to protect pump rooms of tank vessels.

Foam is used for extinguishing flammable liquid fires in boiler and machinery spaces of vessels and also for the protection of pump rooms and cargo tank areas of tank vessels. Proportioning equipment mixes concentrated foam liquid with water from the fire pump making a solution that is piped to nozzles where air is mixed to make the foam. Foam forms a blanket of closely knit bubbles that float on the flammable liquids and smother the fire. An advantage is that the foam blanket remains intact, thus preventing reignition. For deck systems the foam is applied either by turret nozzles or by hand hose line nozzles. Fixed systems are installed in pump rooms and boiler and machinery spaces.

Fig. 32. (A) A fog nozzle applicator. The nozzle valve handle has 3 positions. In forward position, it is ""off."" In middle position (straight up and down) it is for fog. In back position, it is for solid stream. (B) A newer and more versatile nozzle, which is replacing the applicator shown in (A) both in the U.S. Merchant Marine and the U.S. Navy, is this pistol grip nozzle that permits varying the stream. Courtesy Akron Brass Co.

Safety Devices

Protection for breathing is furnished by two related but distinctly different types of equipment. These are the oxygen breathing apparatus and the gas mask, which is now properly called the "air mask respirator." The difference between the two is extremely important, and ignorance may cost you your life. Oxygen breathing apparatus provides an independent source of breathing air that is separate from the air that surrounds you. An air mask respirator simply uses the air that surrounds you. And if there is not enough oxygen in the surrounding air, you will become unconscious and die if you are not rescued.

Oxygen breathing apparatus. Breathing apparatus come in several different configurations, but they all have one thing in common. They all provide an independent source of breathing air that is separate from the air that surrounds you. They can be either: (1) a hose line unit with full-face mask (where you are connected to distant air bottles or pumps via an umbilical air hose; (2) a self-contained breathing apparatus (SCBA) where you carry an air bottle on your back that supplies your face mask; or (3) a pre-placed rescue air pack EEBD (emergency escape breathing device) that consists of a small air bottle (15 minute) connected to a canvas or plastic hood that covers your entire head.

The most common type of breathing apparatus used aboard ships today is the self-contained breathing apparatus (see figure 33). This apparatus provides the wearer with an independent and portable supply of fresh clean air. It consists of a compressed air cylinder mounted into a harness that is worn over the shoulders and fitted with a waist belt. An air hose leads from the bottle valve to a regulator that adjusts air flow

Fig. 33. A self-contained breathing apparatus. This Scott Air Pak is one of several such devices approved by the Coast Guard. At left it is shown properly adjusted by the wearer. When not in use, it is stowed in carrying case.

to a full-face mask. The regulator can be a positive-pressure or demand type. Regulators are also fitted with an emergency bypass that permits air to flow directly from the bottle to the face piece, in case a problem develops in the regulator. Keeping a positive-pressure (over-pressure) air flow in the face mask will help prevent the infiltration of smoke into a poorly adjusted mask; however, care must still be taken to properly tighten all of the straps for the face mask. Modern SCBA units are identical to those worn by many city fire departments. SCBAs have replaced older OBA (oxygen breathing apparatus) for a variety of reasons. OBAs were carried on ships for years because they chemically produced their own oxygen from canisters and thus could be used over and over by simply changing canisters. Now, many ships are fitted with their own air compressor that can refill standard SCBA compressed-air cylinders.

Air mask respirators. Most respirators can be fitted with different types of chemical cartridges for filtering different types of gases or vapors. Other filters, or sometimes pre-filters, are designed to remove only particulate matter from the air by means of a trapping fibrous material. Respirators can be either full-face masks or half-face masks and are tightened snugly about the face with a head strap arrangement. Many companies prohibit crewmen from wearing beards because of respirator wearing requirements. Obviously, the half-face masks do not cover the wearer's eyes and thus will not prevent gases from being absorbed through the eye membranes.

For proper use, the headbands of the mask are adjusted so that the face piece is held very tightly against the face in order to prevent the entrance of gases under the mask. If a respirator is worn incorrectly, it will do the wearer little good. In fact, it may provide the wearer with a false sense of protection and may lead to severe injury. Occupational regulations now require that workmen actually be "fitted" with the proper size of respirator to ensure a good face seal. When wearing a respirator, the wearer can test the tightness of his respirator by covering the filter intakes with his hands and breathing in. If the mask collapses initially and remains so, then the face piece is air tight.

As the respirator wearer inhales, air is brought through the intake canisters and passes through the filter element. Different filter elements are available to chemically filter out selected types of gases or vapors, so be sure to carefully check the type of filter element that your respirator is fitted with. These filter elements can be changed with different filter types to filter out other families of gas. The mask is fitted with a one-way exhaust valve to permit exhaled breath to exit the mask. Masks must be kept clean to ensure proper operation and are usually stored in their own plastic bag for protection and cleanliness. Cleaning is normally accomplished with warm water and mild soap. You can also use a low concentration of medical biocide soap to sanitize the mask.

Air respirators simply purify the air breathed through them and should not be used in an atmosphere containing less than 19% oxygen. If there is any doubt as to the oxygen content of a space or compartment, use an atmosphere tester before entering.

Combustible gas indicators. The presence of combustible gases aboard ship can be detected by a gas chemist or by a ship's officer trained to use a combustible gas indicator. There are several types of gas indicators on the market, and all are very similar. The Drager Detector is shown, and its use is described (fig. 34).

Fig. 34. A combustible gas indicator. The Drager Detector is shown. At the left is case containing several tubes for sampling different types of gas. At right is detector with tube inserted.

The Drager Detector consists of a gas detector pump that is also called the bellows pump, and a glass detector tube that is different for each type of gas to be sampled. Both tips of the glass tube are broken off, and the tube is inserted into the bellows pump. By squeezing the pump a prescribed number of times, the gas that is to be sampled is drawn into the tube. The length of the discoloration of the chemical in the tube indicates the concentration of gas in percentage of volume. If the user has a complete set of detector tubes furnished by the manufacturer, he will be able to detect over 125 different toxic vapors and gases.

Safety line. Before entering a confined space, with either a work respirator or an emergency type of breathing apparatus, the wearer should be attached to a safety line or lifeline device. Some confined space entry procedures will require the worker to wear a special rescue extraction harness. This harness, connected by a small wire to a hand winch, will permit coworkers outside the space to winch out a person in trouble without having to actually enter the confined space themselves.

When using a traditional lifeline, somebody should tend the line to be alert for signals from the entrant. The standard line pull signals should be written on a metal plate on both ends of the line. The memory aid for these signals is **OATH:**

> One pull—**O**k
> Two pulls—**A**dvancing—give slack.
> Three pulls—**T**ake in slack—I'm moving back.
> Four pulls—**H**elp

3. First Aid and
Safe Practices Aboard Ship

First aid, in any situation, consists of the emergency treatment of the sick and/or injured until competent medical or surgical help can be obtained. At sea, however, you may well be the only medical help available.

There are some general rules to keep in mind in almost any emergency situation.

1. Keep the patient lying down until the extent of his injuries can be determined.
2. Check for breathing, bleeding, and signs of shock.
3. Remove only enough clothing to get a clear idea of the extent of the injury.
4. Reassure the casualty. Explain that you have help coming and that everything will be fine.
5. Avoid allowing the casualty to see his or her injury. Even a minor injury may appear severe to the injured person.
6. Never attempt to give an unconscious person anything by mouth, not even water.
7. Do not move the casualty until first aid measures are complete.
8. Always move a casualty feet first, except when going up a ladder.

Before discussing the care of different types of injuries, a few words about *you*. When an injury occurs, whether one or many, excitement and confusion arise. In these situations you will have to force yourself to *keep calm*. Never permit yourself to become overly excited and confused. Act quickly with efficiency and confidence. Doing this will reassure the casualty that everything that can be done is being done.

If there are many casualties, enlist the help of those individuals not seriously injured. This will keep them occupied and from feeling sorry for themselves.

Cardiopulmonary Resuscitation

CPR (cardiopulmonary resuscitation) takes precedence in any illness or injury. If you spend time working on the injury itself, whether bleeding, fracture, wounds, etc., and the casualty is not breathing and his heart is not pumping blood through his veins, you may be patching up a dead person. In short, the first thing to be checked on any casualty is breathing and pulse. This is because if the brain, the computer that tells the rest of the body what to do and how to do it, is without oxygen for a period of 4 to 6 minutes, its cells start to die. These cells can never be regenerated. After about 10 minutes, it is possible that a significant number of brain cells have died so that even if the caregiver is "lucky" enough to get the victim's heart and breathing started, the casualty may already be a "vegetable." Therefore, if breathing and/or pulse are absent, CPR must be started immediately. The procedures for CPR are as follows:

1. Establish an airway. The tongue is the most frequent cause of an airway obstruction (figure 36). When a person is unconscious, the lower jaw relaxes and falls back. The tongue, being attached to the lower jaw, also falls back and blocks the passage of air to the lungs. With certain exceptions, the best way to correct this obstruction is to hyperextend the head, which will thrust the jaw forward, lifting the tongue from the back of the throat, allowing a free flow of air to and from the lungs. This may be all that is needed for the casualty to start breathing on his own. If breathing is in doubt, place your ear over the casualty's mouth so you may feel and/or hear any breathing. If there is no breathing, blow four (4) full deep breaths into the casualty's mouth (hold nose closed), not

allowing the lungs to deflate completely— then check the carotid pulse.

2. A breathing tube is helpful in providing breathing assistance and can assist in clearing the airway while providing some protection to caregiver. A breathing tube is a plastic airway tube that is inserted into the patient's mouth with one end protruding out of the mouth for the use of the caregiver.

3. Check to see if the casualty is still not breathing. Then start mouth-to-mouth artificial ventilation at the rate of one (1) breath every five (5) seconds or twelve (12) times per minute until spontaneous breathing starts.

4. Check carotid pulse to see if the heart is beating (see figure 37). The carotid arteries are on either side of the "Adam's apple." Place two fingers on the Adam's apple and slide them to the cleft on either side and press lightly to feel the pulse. If you do not feel a pulse, start artificial circulation by placing the heel of your hand on the lower half of the sternum (breastbone), not the xyphoid, which is the very tip of the sternum. Compress the chest $1\frac{1}{2}$ to 2 inches.

   Compress the chest at the rate of 80 to 100 times per minute. This is done by compressing the chest 15 times, then giving 2 full ventilations (breaths) into the casualty until he becomes conscious or the heart starts beating on its own and spontaneous breathing returns.

The Coast Guard requires that all licensed officers be certified in CPR. This must be renewed every two years, and is particularly important because if there have been any changes in the recommended procedures, the individual will learn them when he updates his certificate. Although nonlicensed personnel are not required to have CPR training, it is strongly recommended that able seamen also receive certification. A shipmate's life may be saved.

Near Drowning

Drowning or near drowning is caused by asphyxiation due to submersion. All near-drowning victims suffer from acute asphyxia. There is a lowering of arterial oxygen (hypoxemia), and an increase in the metabolic acidosis that persists in those who have aspirated fluid.

It is useless to attempt to drain water from the lungs of either a freshwater or a sea water near-drowning victim. However, placing the patient in the Trendelenburg position (head and shoulders lower than the abdomen and pelvis), may promote drainage.

Often victims of submersion swallow water, which fills the stomach and prevents movement of the diaphragm. Roll the victim face down and lift him just anterior to the pelvis. Any water will drain out of his stomach by gravity.

Roll the victim over and begin the routine CPR as follows:

1. Establish an airway (fig. 35).
2. Check carotid pulse (fig. 36).
3. Start closed chest cardiac massage, alternating with positive pressure mouth-to-mouth ventilation.

	In Respiratory Arrest	*In Cardiac Arrest*
CAUSES	Airway obstruction Respiratory depression Cardiac arrest	Cardiac standstill Ventricular fibrillation Circulatory collapse
SYMPTOMS	Absence of respiration Cyanosis Dilated pupils	Absence of pulses Absence of respiration Dilated pupils
TREATMENT	Airway opened Breathing restored Circulation restored Definitive medical treatment sought	

Fig. 35. The airway. The two sketches on the left show patient when assistance first arrives on scene. Lower jaw is relaxed, and passage of air to the lungs is blocked. Sketches on right show how airway is opened by hyperextending the head. This is the first step in the administration of CPR (cardiopulmonary resuscitation). CPR has taken the place of all older forms of reviving the unconscious or apparently drowned.

Fig. 36. The carotid pulse.

Hypothermia

Survival in water has been a problem plaguing seamen for hundreds of years. In cold water this problem is increased because without heat the body functions soon deteriorate. Numbness, loss of muscle control, and loss of consciousness are the symptoms of hypothermia.

The loss of body heat and subsequent reduction of body temperature can occur either in cold water or when exposed to cold air. If survival ashore in a cold atmosphere is going to be necessary for any length of time, the seaman should particularly avoid getting wet if at all possible. Layers of heavy clothing help insulate the body and prevent loss of heat.

Water is of much higher density than air and thus conducts heat away from the body much more rapidly than is the case with air. If clothing is porous, it does little to reduce the flow of heat. Nonporous clothing such as foul-weather gear or an exposure suit are preferred if exposure to cold is expected. The body should be kept in a tightly coiled position when in cold water to reduce surface contact and thus heat loss. Attempts to swim generally only compound the heat loss problem. Contrary to general belief, alcohol *increases* the rate of body heat loss.

The seaman should remember the following if he expects to survive in cold water:

1. Wear nonporous clothing if available. Foul-weather gear helps, but is not a replacement for an immersion suit.
2. Stay in water no longer than absolutely necessary.
3. Keep calm and keep body tightly coiled to reduce body heat loss (knees tucked up to chin).
4. Wear a life jacket.

The treatment for hypothermia victims is as follows:

1. Remove wet clothing.
2. Cover with warm blankets or have another person keep the victim warm by lying on top of or beside him.

3. Give stimulating drinks such as hot coffee or tea. Do not give alcohol.
4. Get the victim to a proper medical facility as soon as possible.
5. Handle the victim gently and with extreme care. His flesh may damage easily.

Management of Wounds and Injuries

By definition, a wound is a break in the continuity of body tissues involving an opening in the skin, and an injury is the disruption in the continuity of body tissues not necessarily involving the skin. With this in mind, you can see that all wounds may be classified as injuries, but not all injuries may be classified as wounds.

In wound prophylaxis keeping the break clean is of utmost importance. This can be accomplished by doing the following:

1. Make sure your hands are clean. Scrub them thoroughly with soap and hot water.
2. Place a piece of sterile bandage over the wound while cleaning the surrounding area.
3. If the wound is in a hairy area, shave the hair off 2 to 3 inches around the wound. (Never shave off any part of the eyebrow, as it may not grow back.)
4. If possible, flush the wound thoroughly with sterile saline solution. This will wash out any loose debris.
5. Apply a dry sterile dressing, using only sufficient pressure to stop bleeding.
6. If the casualty has not had a tetanus booster within the past six months, give 0.5 cc. of tetanus toxoid, injected into the arm to prevent "lock-jaw."
7. Start antibiotic therapy as indicated.

Control of Hemorrhage

Hemorrhage, or bleeding, is the escape of blood from arteries, veins, and capillaries because of a break in their walls. Control of active bleeding is urgent.

While external bleeding is very apparent, internal bleeding can be just as serious. The following symptoms will usually be present in both types of hemorrhage, but perhaps disregarded in external bleeding:

1. Pale skin or pale mucous membranes.
2. Subnormal temperature.
3. Increased pulse rate or feeling feeble and easily compressed or lost.
4. Blood pressure lowered.
5. Dilated pupils, slow in reacting to light.
6. Ringing in ears.
7. Faintness or fainting (may be first symptom).
8. Thirst due to dehydration.
9. Air hunger (yawning).
10. Impaired vision.

The treatment of internal hemorrhage can be accomplished only by surgery. Until a patient reaches a hospital, he must be kept alive with the aid of I.V.s (blood volume expanders), that can be used until whole blood is available at the hospital. Blood loss can produce hemorrhagic shock.

For external hemorrhage the steps for control are the following:

1. Local pressure by use of pressure dressings.
2. The use of a tourniquet, a constricting bond that can be placed around an extremity and tightened until the escaping blood flow stops. It should be used only as a last resort.

Management of Shock

Shock is a state of circulatory deficiency associated with depression of the vital processes of the body. The symptoms of shock are the following:

1. Eyes are glassy, lackluster; pupils are dilated; patient shows fear and/or apprehension.

2. Breathing is shallow and irregular.
3. Lips may be pale or cyanotic (bluish grey).
4. Skin is pale, cool, and moist or waxy.

The treatment for shock patients includes the following:

1. Keep patient lying on his or her back.
2. Raise feet 10 to 12 inches higher than head.
3. Keep patient warm by removing wet clothing and by covering with a blanket.
4. Ascertain cause of the shock and contact a physician.

Management of Burns

Burns are classified in several ways: by the extent of body surface burned, by the depth of the burn, and by the causative agent. Of these, extent of body surface burned plays the greatest role in survival. This is calculated by what is called the "Rule of Nines" (fig. 37).

Using this as a basis, an adult having 15 percent of body surface burned, or a small child having 10 percent of body surface burned, can go into shock. If more than 20 percent of body surface is burned, it can endanger life. If 30 percent or more of body surface is burned, it is usually fatal.

Keeping the above in mind while adding another factor, classification of depth or degree, will help determine the mortality rate of burn injuries.

First-degree burns involve only the outer layer of skin or epidermis. Mild sunburn is a good example.

Second-degree burns extend through the epidermis and involve the inner layers of skin or dermis, but not enough to prevent rapid regeneration of the skin. They are characterized by blisters and moderately severe pain.

Third-degree burns destroy both the epidermis and dermis along with underlying tissues. Severe pain may be absent because nerve endings have been destroyed. The color may range from white and lifeless, as in scalds, to black and charred, as in thermal or gas explosions. Skin grafts are generally required before complete healing can take place.

If the burn involves 20 percent or less of body surface burned, immerse the part in ice water. Where immersion is impractical, repeated applications of ice-cold moist towels to the burned area are advisable. Continue this ice-water treatment until no pain is felt. This could take anywhere from 30 minutes to 5 hours.

Treatment for pain of a first-degree burn should require no more than 1 or 2 aspirins for relief of discomfort; for moderately severe pain, as with second-degree burns, codeine ½ grain (32 mg.) orally or by injection; for pain from extensive burns (third-degree), 8 to 20 mg. of morphine injected subcu-

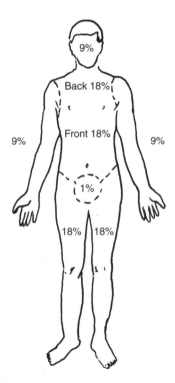

Fig. 37. "Rule of Nines" for analysis of burn treatment. Head = 9%, front of body = 18%, genital area = 1%, each leg = 18%.

taneously. Morphine should not be injected intramuscularly because of the probability of reduced peripheral circulation and possible morphine poisoning.

In burns as with other things that happen to, and within, the body, the body's own mechanisms take over and try to help right the wrong. In the case of burns, the body rushes fluid in the form of plasma to the site of the burn to help cool it. This causes a loss of fluid in other important parts of the body, including the blood stream. With a decrease in blood volume, shock is imminent. Therefore, these fluids must be replaced. If the casualty is conscious, he may be given liquids (coffee, tea, water, etc.) with salt added (about $\frac{1}{4}$ teaspoon to 8 ounces). If unconscious, an I.V. of sterile normal saline should be started (8 to 10 drops per minute).

Safe Practices

Observing the following practices will help avoid accidents and injuries aboard merchant ships.

> Work clothes should fit well and be in good repair. Any loose dangling parts can catch on machinery or fittings. Pants cuffs should not be used on trousers. Safety shoes can prevent injury to toes from falling objects. Composition traction soles help prevent slips and falls on wet or oily decks. Gloves with gauntlets can easily get caught when handling lines on a warping head.

> Goggles should be worn anytime there is danger of injury to the eyes. Activities potentially dangerous include chipping paint or rust, sharpening tools on a power wheel, or letting go the anchor.

> Only safety shackles with locknuts and cotter pins should be used aloft. Shackles used elsewhere should be wired whenever there is danger that the pin may tend to back out.

> Bridles or slings for pontoons or hatch beams should have lanyards secured at each end above hooks so that there is no need to endanger hands or fingers. When using

hydraulic or mechanical hatch openings, be sure safety
hooks are locked and pinned. When opening or closing
hatches, be sure all hands stand well clear.

Don't stand in the bight of a line.

Whether on deck or dockside, be alert for cargo operations. Do not walk near cargo operations until the long-
shore signalman indicates that it is safe to do so.

Don't leave manholes, floor plates, or hatches open without stanchions and guard ropes in place. Use lights and
a warning sign to keep the unwary from straying into
danger.

Don't cover open or partly open hatches with tarpaulins.

Use a hardhat when working cargo or when a member of a
lifeboat crew.

When only one section of hatch is being worked, hatch
beams or pontoons that can be hit by drafts of cargo or
caught by hooks should be secured by locking devices
or lashed in position. No one should stand on a section
of an open hatch during cargo operations.

Compartments that have been closed for a long time, especially tanks or double bottoms, should be checked
and found "gas free" and with sufficient oxygen before
anyone is allowed to enter.

Cleaning compounds must be used with care and instructions read to be sure that injury to eyes or skin will not
occur. Such substances as lye, boiler compounds, oxalic
acid, caustic soda, etc., should be used with care. Some
detergents can cause rapid rotting of ropes used for
bos'n's chairs or stages.

Before men go aloft or over the side, gantlines, blocks,
stages, etc., should be tested. Tests are simple and
need little time.

Make sure the electricity is turned off before working on a
constant tension winch. Should your clothes get caught
between the warping head and the mooring line, you
may be seriously injured or killed.

Compartments being painted should be well ventilated.
Crew using spray painting gear should have respira-
tory protection, face masks, filters, etc.

Never smoke while lying down in your bunk. Don't smoke near open hatches. Don't toss cigarettes or ashes out of portholes. They can blow back aboard, down ventilators, or burn through tarpaulins and start fires in a hold.

Secure pilot ladders to padeyes on deck, not to chain or pipe rails. Ladders must be checked to see that all slack is out by putting weight on them while keeping a firm grip before the pilot comes aboard or departs the ship.

Before going up the stack near a whistle, ask permission from the mate on watch.

Before going up the masts near the radio antennae, get permission from the mate on watch and inform the radio officer. Avoid standing close to a radio or radar antenna in operation.

Aloft, over the side, or going up or down ladders, remember: "One hand for the ship, one for yourself."

Remember that the wise seaman always wears a belt with his dungarees or other work pants. Otherwise, his shipmate who reaches to grab him when he slips and starts to go over the side may wind up holding only an empty pair of pants.

Use a flashlight in dark areas. Do not use a match. Always walk with a flashlight in dimly lit areas. Don't show lights in a way that will blind the lookout on the bow or the mate on the bridge.

Stepladders or straight ladders used aboard ship should be lashed in place. Lanyards fitted near the upper end are useful for this purpose. The use of hooks on ladders has caused many accidents.

Ensure that electric tools are grounded before use.

Lift with legs and thigh muscles. Do not lift with your back.

Remember that oily decks cause slips. This is a frequent cause of injury.

Help protect beaches and wildlife—don't dump or throw overboard oil or oily waste. Don't dump garbage. International regulations allow dumping of wet garbage out three miles; however, it is best not to dump at all.

Do not overstress any line, particularly synthetic line. If a synthetic line parts, it lashes out with the greatest force.

The windlass should not be left in gear. Do not take it out of gear until the brake is secure.

Always return a fire extinguisher to its proper location.

Do not leave a fire extinguisher in an empty condition. Turn it in to the bos'n or chief mate.

Never use defective electrical equipment.

Do not use fire hoses for any purpose other than firefighting or fire drills.

Do not handle wire without gloves. Work gloves should be loose fitting and easily removed.

Do not make stage lines or manropes fast to a pipe rail or removable section of rail.

When handling a rope or wire on a warping head, make sure someone is at the controls of the winch.

Be very careful surging synthetic rope on a bitt because it can fuse. It is much better practice to slack back on the winch.

Ensure that snatch blocks and shackles are stronger than the rope or wire with which they will be used.

When handling blocks under strain, keep fingers out of the way of falls, sheaves, and hooks. This is particularly important when hooking on a lifeboat.

Use a marlinespike to help lining up bolt holes.

Never leave a load suspended from a boom head.

Use the proper clamps to secure a fall to a winch drum.

Haul a crew member aloft by hand, not by winch.

Make sure that all tools taken aloft have lanyards. They should be carried in a bucket.

Use a line to lower a light into a hold or tank. Do not lower it by its own cable.

If you are going to leave a cluster light in a cargo hold, ensure that it is disconnected.

4. Able Seaman

The following information concerning requirements and certification as an able seaman is reproduced from the *Code of Federal Regulations: Title 46—Shipping*, Subpart 12.05 (Washington, D.C.: U.S. Government Printing Office, 2003). Standards of Training, Certification, and Watchkeeping for Seafarers (STCW) certification is also required for able seamen who intend to work on vessels offshore or in foreign service. The STCW competencies from the International Marine Organization (IMO) code are included in appendix A of this manual. The term used internationally is "rating forming part of the navigation watch."

Subpart 12.05—Able Seaman

Sec. 12.05-1 Certification required.

(a) Every person employed in a rating as able seaman on any United States vessel requiring certificated able seamen, before signing articles of agreement, shall present to the master, his or her certificate as able seaman (issued in the form of a merchant mariner's document).

(b) No certificate as able seaman is required of any person employed on any tug or towboat on the bays and sounds connected directly with the seas, or on any unrigged vessel except seagoing barges or tank barges.

(c) The following categories of able seaman are established:

(1) Able Seaman—Any Waters, Unlimited.

(2) Able Seaman—Limited.

(3) Able Seaman—Special.

(4) Able Seaman—Special (OSV).
[CGD 80-131, 45 FR 69240, Oct. 20, 1980]

Sec. 12.05-3 General requirements.

(a) To qualify for certification as able seaman an applicant must.

(1) Be at least 18 years of age;

(2) Pass the prescribed physical examination;

(3) Meet the sea service or training requirements set forth in this part;

(4) Pass an examination demonstrating ability as an able seaman and lifeboatman; and,

(5) Speak and understand the English language as would be required in performing the general duties of able seaman and during an emergency aboard ship.

(b) An STCW endorsement valid for any period on or after February 1, 2002, will be issued or renewed only when the candidate for certification as an able seaman also produces satisfactory evidence, on the basis of assessment of a practical demonstration of skills and abilities, of having achieved or maintained within the previous 5 years the minimum standards of competence for the following 4 areas of basic safety:

(1) Personal survival techniques as set out in table A-VI/1-1 of the STCW Code (incorporated by reference in Sec. 12.01-3).

(2) Fire prevention and fire-fighting as set out in table A-VI/1-2 of the STCW Code.

(3) Elementary first aid as set out in table A-VI/1-3 of the STCW Code.

(4) Personal safety and social responsibilities as set out in table A-VI/1-4 of the STCW Code.

(c) An STCW endorsement valid for any period on or after February 1, 2002, will be issued or renewed only when the candidate for certification as able seamen meets the requirements of STCW Regulation II/4 and of Section A-II/4 of the STCW Code, if the candidate will be serving as a rating forming part of the navigational watch on a seagoing ship of 500 GT or more.

[CGD 80-131, 45 FR 69240, Oct. 20, 1980, as amended by CGD 95-062, 62 FR 34537, June 26, 1997; CGD 95-062, 62 FR 40140, July 25, 1997; USCG-1999- 5610, 67 FR 66068, Oct. 30, 2002]

Sec. 12.05-5 Physical requirements.

(a) All applicants for a certificate of service as able seaman shall be required to pass a physical examination given by a medical officer of the United States Public Health Service and present to the Officer in Charge, Marine Inspection, a certificate executed by the Public Health Service Officer. Such certificate shall attest to the applicant's acuity of vision, color sense, hearing, and general physical condition. In exceptional cases where an applicant would be put to great inconvenience or expense to appear before a medical officer of the United States Public Health Service, the physical examination and certification may be made by any other reputable physician.

(b) The medical examination for an able seaman is the same as for an original license as a deck officer as set forth in Sec. 10.205 of this subchapter. If the applicant is in possession of an unexpired deck license, the Officer in Charge, Marine Inspection, may waive the requirement for a physical examination.

[CGFR 65-50, 30 FR 16640, Dec. 30, 1965, as amended by USCG-1998-4442, 63 FR 52189, Sept. 30, 1998]

Sec. 12.05-7 Service or training requirements.

(a) The minimum service required to qualify an applicant for the various categories of able seaman is as listed in this paragraph.

(1) Able Seaman—Any Waters, Unlimited. Three years service on deck on vessels operating on the oceans or the Great Lakes.

(2) Able Seaman—Limited. Eighteen months service on deck in vessels of 100 gross tons or over which operate in a service not exclusively confined to the rivers and smaller inland lakes of the United States.

(3) Able Seaman—Special. Twelve months service on deck on vessels operating on the oceans, or the navigable waters of the United States including the Great Lakes.

(4) Able Seaman—Special (OSV). Six months service on deck on vessels operating on the oceans, or the navigable waters of the United States including the Great Lakes.

(5) After July 31, 1998, to receive an STCW endorsement for service as a "rating forming part of a navigational watch" on a seagoing ship of 500 GT or more, the applicant's seagoing service must include training and experience associated with navigational watchkeeping and involve the performance of duties carried out under the direct supervision of the master, the officer in charge of the navigational watch, or a qualified rating forming part of a navigational watch. The training and experience must be sufficient to establish that the candidate has achieved the standard of competence prescribed in table A-II/4 of the STCW Code (incorporated by reference in Sec. 12.01-3), in accordance with the methods of demonstrating competence and the criteria for evaluating competence specified in that table.

Note: Employment considerations for the various categories of able seaman are contained in Sec. 157.20-15 of this chapter.

(b) Training programs approved by the Commanding Officer, National Maritime Center, may be substituted for the required periods of service on deck as follows:

(1) A graduate of a school ship may be rated as able seaman upon satisfactory completion of the course of instruction. For this purpose, *school ship* is interpreted to mean an institution which offers a complete course of instruction, including a period of at sea training, in the skills appropriate to the rating of able seaman.

(2) Training programs, other than those classified as a school ship, may be substituted for up to one third of the required service on deck. The service/training ratio for each program is determined by the Commanding Officer, National Maritime Center, who may allow a maximum of three days on deck service credit for each day of instruction.

(c) A certificate of service as *Able Seaman, Great Lakes— 18 months' service,* is considered equivalent to a certificate of service as *Able Seaman—Limited.*

(d) A certificate of service as Able Seaman with the following route, vessel, or time restrictions is considered equivalent to a certificate of service as *Able Seaman—Special:*

(1) Any waters—12 months.

(2) Tugs and towboats—any waters.

(3) Bays and sounds—12 months, vessels 500 gross tons or under not carrying passengers.

(4) Seagoing barges—12 months.

(e) An individual holding a certificate of service endorsed as noted in paragraphs (c) or (d) of this section may have his or her merchant mariner's document endorsed with the equivalent category, upon request.

[CGD 80-131, 45 FR 69240, Oct. 20, 1980, as amended by CGD 95-072, 60 FR 50460, Sept. 29, 1995; CGD 95-062, 62 FR 34537, June 26, 1997; CGD 95-062, 62 FR 40140, July 25, 1997; USCG-1998-4442, 63 FR 52189, Sept. 30, 1998; USCG-1999-5610, 67 FR 66068, Oct. 30, 2002]

Sec. 12.05-9 Examination and demonstration of ability.

(a) Before an applicant is certified as an able seaman, he or she shall prove to the satisfaction of the Coast Guard by oral or other means of examination, and by actual demonstration, his or her knowledge of seamanship and the ability to carry out effectively all the duties that may be required of an able seaman, including those of a lifeboatman. The applicant shall demonstrate that he or she:

(1) Has been trained in all the operations connected with the launching of lifeboats and liferafts, and in the use of oars;

(2) Is acquainted with the practical handling of boats; and

(3) Is capable of taking command of the boat's crew.

(b) The examination, whether administered orally or by other means, must be conducted only in the English language and must consist of questions regarding:

(1) Lifeboats and liferafts, the names of their essential parts, and a description of the required equipment;

(2) The clearing away, swinging out, and lowering of lifeboats and liferafts, and handling of lifeboats under oars and

sails, including questions relative to the proper handling of a boat in a heavy sea;

(3) The operation and functions of commonly used types of davits;

(4) The applicant's knowledge of nautical terms; boxing the compass, either by degrees or points according to his experience; running lights, passing signals, and fog signals for vessels on the high seas, in inland waters, or on the Great Lakes depending upon the waters on which the applicant has had service; and distress signals; and,

(5) The applicant's knowledge of commands in handling the wheel by obeying orders passed to him as *wheelsman,* and knowledge of the use of engineroom telegraph or bell-pull signals.

(c) In the actual demonstration, the applicant shall show his ability by taking command of a boat and directing the operation of clearing away, swinging out, lowering the boat into the water, and acting as coxswain in charge of the boat under oars. He shall demonstrate his ability to row by actually pulling an oar in the boat. He shall also demonstrate knowledge of the principal knots, bends, splices, and hitches in common use by actually making them.

(c-1) The applicant must demonstrate to the satisfaction of the Officer in Charge, Marine Inspection, his knowledge of pollution laws and regulations, procedures for discharge containment and cleanup, and methods for disposal of sludge and waste material from cargo and fueling operations.

(d) Any person who is in valid possession of a certificate as able seaman endorsed, *any waters—12 months* and who can produce documentary evidence of sufficient service to qualify for a certificate as able seaman endorsed, *any waters—unlimited,* may be issued a new document bearing this endorsement without additional professional examination. The applicant shall surrender for cancellation the document bearing the limited endorsement. No physical examination will be required at the time of this exchange unless it is found that the applicant obviously suffers from some physical or mental infirmity to a degree that in the opinion of the Officer in Charge, Marine Inspection, would render him incompetent to perform the usual duties of an able seaman at sea. If such condition is believed to exist, the applicant shall be required to undergo an examination by a medical officer of the Public Health Service to determine his competency.

[CGFR 65-50, 30 FR 16640, Dec. 30, 1965, as amended by CGD 71-161R, 37 FR 28263, Dec. 21, 1972; CGD 94-029, 61 FR 47064, Sept. 6, 1996; USCG- 2002-13058, 67 FR 61278, Sept. 30, 2002]

Sec. 12.05-11 General provisions respecting merchant mariner's document endorsed for service as able seamen.

(a) The holder of a merchant mariner's document endorsed for the rating of able seamen may serve in any unlicensed rating in the deck department without obtaining an additional endorsement; *provided*, however, that the holder shall hold the appropriate endorsement under the STCW (incorporated by reference in Sec. 12.01-3) when serving in as a "rating forming part of a navigational watch" on a seagoing ship of 500 GT or more.

(b) A merchant mariner's document endorsed as able seaman will also be considered a certificate of efficiency as lifeboatman without further endorsement.

(c) This type of document will describe clearly the type of able seaman certificate which it represents, e.g.: able seaman—any waters; able seaman—any waters, 12 months; able seaman—Great Lakes, 18 months; able seaman—on freight vessels, 500 gross tons or less on bays or sounds, and on tugs, towboats, and barges on any waters.

[CGFR 65-50, 30 FR 16640, Dec. 30, 1965, as amended by CGD 95-062, 62 FR 34537, June 26, 1997; USCG-1999-5610, 67 FR 66068, Oct. 30, 2002]

Topics to Be Mastered

There are many books that will help seamen to improve their knowledge of their job. While some tasks can be easily made clear by practical experience, a combination of study and on-the-job work is the best way of becoming skilled. The following information does not try to cover the whole field, but sets forth some of the things sailors have to know to do their work safely and efficiently.

Anchor and Anchor Chain

Practically all ships of any size use the patent or stockless anchor, which is shown in figure 38. Although the old-fashioned or admiralty anchor is still unmatched in holding power ton for ton, it is rarely seen today because it is clumsy and awkward to use. A ship's anchor will weigh roughly 1 to 1½ pounds for each ton of a vessel's displacement. An anchor works like a pick axe. When driven into the ground, the pick will require a tremendous amount of force to pull it loose with a straight pull on the handle. By lifting the handle, however, a leverage is obtained that breaks it free. An anchor holds because a long cable causes the pull on the anchor to be in line with the shank. To break the anchor free, the cable is taken in. This lifts the shank of the anchor, producing a leverage that loosens its hold.

The large, heavy chains that hold the anchors are called anchor cables. The length of a ship's cable is standardized by the American Bureau of Shipping and is based on length,

Fig. 38. A Baldt stockless anchor. Courtesy Baldt, Inc.

breadth, tonnage, and freeboard of the vessel. The chain is divided into "shots," which are connected by detachable links and are 15 fathoms in length. Since a fathom is 6 feet in length, a shot is equal to 90 feet.

The anchor cable is marked both by paint and turns of wire at each shot as follows:

1 shot—1 turn of wire on first stud from each side of the detachable link and white paint on the stud link on either side of the detachable link.

2 shots—2 turns of wire on the second stud from each side of the detachable link and white paint on the 2 stud links on either side of the detachable link.

3 shots—3 turns of wire on the third stud from each side of the detachable link and white paint on the 3 stud links on either side of the detachable link.

For each additional shot one more turn of wire is added and one more stud link on either side of the detachable link is added.

Compasses

There are two basic types of compasses. Most commercial vessels have a gyrocompass, and lifeboats are required to have a magnetic compass. The gyrocompass indicates true north and derives its directive force from the rotation of a motor-driven gyroscope. The magnetic compass derives its directive force from the earth's natural magnetic field.

Gyrocompass. As a mechanical-electrical device that requires ship's power to function, the gyrocompass only needs minor correction and points very close to true north. However, it is subject to mechanical breakdown, precession, high latitude errors, and improper speed and latitude settings. These errors can be significant. The gyrocompass must be checked frequently by azimuths and by comparison with the magnetic compass.

Magnetic compass. The standard compass on a ship is a magnetic compass and it serves as a backup for the gyrocompass. (The standard compass course is usually abbreviated "psc," per standard compass.) It is located as high as possible in the ship to eliminate as much of the ship's magnetic field upon it as possible. Magnetic compasses must be corrected to eliminate error called deviation caused by the steel in the structure of the ship or boat. After this error is compensated for, or corrected, the magnetic compass points approximately to magnetic north. This differs from true north by variation, which is the difference between magnetic north and true north. Variation is different in all locations and is generally given on the navigational chart (fig. 39).

Compass courses. Compass courses on merchant ships are given in degrees. Boxing the compass helps give a sense of direction. The table on page 119 gives the direction by degrees as well as by points. There are 32 points, of which four (N, S, E, and W) are cardinal and four (NE, SE, SW, and NW) are intercardinal. Each point equals 11¼ degrees. Quarter points (for example N¼ E) are rarely, if ever, used today.

Buoyage

The able seaman should have a rudimentary knowledge of the buoyage system used in the United States. Further information can be found in Bowditch or *Dutton's* (see References, p. 174). The following, however, is basic:

When entering a channel from the sea, red nun buoys will be on the starboard side, green can buoys will be on the

Fig. 39. Standard 7.5 inch magnetic compass.

Name	Points	Degrees
North	0	0° 0′0″
N by E	1	11° 15′
NNE	2	22° 30′
NE by N	3	33° 45′
NE	4	45° 00′
NE by E	5	56° 15′
ENE	6	67° 30′
E by N	7	78° 45′
East	8	90° 00′
E by S	9	101° 15′
ESE	10	112° 30′
SE by E	11	123° 45′
SE	12	135° 00′
SE by S	13	146° 15′
SSE	14	157° 30′
S by E	15	168° 45′
South	16	180° 00′
S by W	17	191° 15′
SSW	18	202° 30′
SW by S	19	213° 45′
SW	20	225° 00′
SW by W	21	236° 15′
WSW	22	247° 30′
W by S	23	258° 45′
West	24	270° 00′
W by N	25	281° 15′
WNW	26	292° 30′
NW by W	27	303° 45′
NW	28	315° 00′
NW by N	29	326° 15′
NNW	30	337° 30′
N by W	31	348° 45′
North	32	360° 00′

port side. If lighted buoys are used, lights on starboard
side will be red, lights on port side will be green.

When entering a channel from the sea, numbers increase
numerically as land is approached (2, 4, 6, etc.). Red
buoys have even numbers, green buoys have odd numbers.

Midchannel buoys are vertically striped red and white. If
lighted, the light will be white.

Steering

The first thing you must know when learning to steer is that
the ship's head, indicated by the lubber line, moves, while
the compass *always* points to north. The job is to bring the
lubber line back to the degree marking that is the desired
course. It may help to remember: "Come right to add. Come
left to subtract." For example, if steering course 250° and ordered to come to course 270°, apply right rudder or add 20°.
"Right rudder" means turn the wheel to the right or clockwise. "Left rudder" means turn the wheel left or counterclockwise.

When at the helm do not keep a knife or wrench in your
pocket because the iron in them will cause an error in the
magnetic compass.

When steering in rough weather, the ship may yaw and
roll without getting seriously off course. The halfway point
between the compass headings at the ends of the roll or yaw
is the course being steered.

A skilled helmsman—or quartermaster—steers with the
least possible amount of rudder to maintain the course. Too
much rudder cuts down the speed and wastes fuel. Whether
steering or standing by on the bridge when the automatic pilot is being used, the helmsman should help the watch officer
to see that the ship is on course and that the rudder is being
used properly. Remember that if on autopilot, the proper
"rudder" and "weather" adjustments must be used. A con-
tributing factor to the *Exxon Valdez* disaster may have been
that those in authority on the bridge forgot that the ship was
on autopilot. In the confusion of the emergency, when the

helmsman spun the wheel to make a radical course change, he was only changing course a small amount for each revolution of the wheel. He was not placing the rudder hard left or hard right.

A wheelsman should check the gyro steering repeater against the magnetic steering compass at least once every fifteen minutes. The gyro, being mechanical, can go wrong, and this simple check will show up errors. Together with the watch officer, the wheelsman should check the steering compass against the standard magnetic compass at least each hour and after a course change. Repeaters and the master gyro should also be checked at regular intervals. When the wheel is relieved, it is customary to tell the officer on watch the course being steered before leaving the bridge. This practice serves to help avoid errors.

When steering by landmarks, it is best to use those far away. Closer landmarks open rapidly on the bow as the ship gets near. When steering at night by stars, remember the stars change in direction as they move across the sky; so refer to the compass every few minutes.

Commands to the helmsman. A good helmsman learns the steering commands so well that they become second nature to him. A few of the more basic commands are given below:

Right (left) 5°, 10°, 15°, etc., rudder—Turn the wheel to the right (left) until the rudder is placed at the number of degrees ordered. This command is frequently used in making a change of course. The helmsman would then be ordered to steer the new course by such a command as "Steady on course_____°" in time to permit him to "meet her" on the new course. The complete command would be: "Right 10° rudder, steady on course 275°."

Give her more rudder—Increase the rudder angle. The command is given with the rudder already over when it is desired to make the ship turn more rapidly. The command should be followed by the exact number of degrees desired for the turn.

Meet her—Use rudder as necessary to check the swing. This command is given when the ship is nearing the desired course.

Ease the rudder to 15°, 10°, 5°, etc.—Decrease the rudder angle. The command is given when the ship is nearing its new heading, and it is desired to slow the swing.

Steady, steady as you go—Steer the course that the ship is heading when you receive the command. This command is given when, in changing course, the new course is reached or the ship is heading as desired.

Rudder amidships—Place the rudder amidships. The command may be given when the ship is turning, and it is desired to make her swing less rapidly.

Shift your rudder—Change from right to left rudder (or vice versa), an equal amount.

Mind your rudder—A warning that the ship is swinging to the right (left) of the ordered course because of bad steering. Pay attention!

Nothing to the right (left)—Do not let the ship's head move to the right (left) of the ordered course. This command is frequently used in a narrow channel.

How does she head?—A question to the helmsman. He should give the ship's head at the time. "200°, sir."

Keep her so—A command to the helmsman when he reports the ship's heading, and it is desired that he steady the ship down on that heading.

Very well—An acknowledgment from the master or conning officer after the helmsman has reported that an order has been carried out. It is never used by the helmsman. "Very well" is used rather than "all right," which might be confused with a command to use right rudder.

Come right (left) to course 120° [or whatever]—Put the rudder over right (left) and steady on course ordered.

Lookout. One of the most important jobs required of a seaman is standing lookout watch. When an object is reported, the bearing should be given accurately so that the captain or mate on watch can look in the right direction and see it. Since there is rarely a compass available to the lookout, he will make his report using relative bearings as shown in figure 40. It is important that the lookout line himself up with the ship's centerline so that he will make an accurate report. If it is daytime, it is helpful if he points.

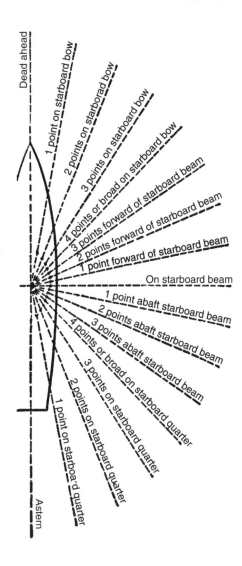

Fig. 40. Relative bearings from a ship.

On some vessels the lookout strikes bells on the half hour to indicate the passage of time, although this custom has fallen into disuse. During darkness the lookout checks the navigation lights every half hour and reports whether they are burning brightly or not.

If there is no telephone at the bow station, it is customary to indicate objects sighted on the starboard side with one stroke of the bell, objects sighted on the port side with two strokes, and objects dead ahead with three strokes.

An attentive lookout on the bow can often see objects in the water not easily seen by the officer on the bridge. Although the watch officer will scan the horizon frequently, he does have other duties. Therefore, the lookout should report everything he sees. This includes other vessels, navigational aids, discolored water, objects in the water, or anything unusual. It is better to report too much than too little. A lookout cannot allow his attention to be distracted. He cannot be assigned any other jobs. The safety of the ship is in his hands.

Lead Line

Merchant ships are equipped with fathometers or Doppler speed logs that register the depth of water, but seamen still have occasional use for the lead line and must be familiar with its use. The hand lead weighs about 7 to 14 pounds and is marked as indicated in figure 41.

The lead has its bottom hollowed out so that tallow or soap can be put in it to bring back a sample of the bottom. This process is called "arming the lead." If a ship or boat is going ahead, the lead must be swung forward to obtain an up and down cast. Fathoms marked on the lead line are called "marks." The intermediate whole fathoms are called "deeps." In reporting depths it is customary to use these terms as "by the mark five," "deep six," etc. The only fractions of a fathom usually reported are halves and quarters, the customary expression being "and a half, eight," "less a quarter, four," etc.

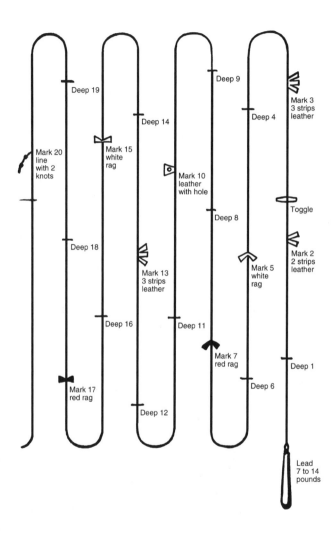

Fig. 41. The markings of a handlead line.

Blocks and Tackles

Blocks are one of the most important fittings aboard ship. They are made of wood, metal, or synthetic materials and their construction and use should be thoroughly understood. When you are being lowered away in a lifeboat, your life and safety depend upon the blocks in the lifeboat falls. The parts of a wooden block are shown in figure 42. The frame is also known as the shell. The opening between the shell and the top of the sheave is known as the swallow.

Blocks take their name from the number of sheaves; a single block has 1 sheave, a double block has 2, and so on. They are identified by their shape or construction and also by the use or place they occupy aboard ship. The size of the block is governed by the size of the rope to be used with it. The length of a wooden block in inches should be about 3 times the circumference of the fiber rope to be used with it. Blocks for use with wire rope are not so well standardized, but the general Coast Guard rule is that the diameter of the sheave should be 20 times the diameter of the wire.

A tackle or purchase is an assembly of ropes (falls) and blocks used to multiply power or to gain a better lead, as in the use of a single whip, making it easier to handle light loads but

Fig. 42. Parts of a typical wood-framed block.

gaining no power or mechanical advantage. If the whip is reversed and the block is attached to the weight to be moved, the whip is then called a runner, and the mechanical advantage or power is doubled. An easy way to determine the mechanical advantage is to count the number of parts of line supporting the movable block. A tackle is said to be rigged "to advantage" when hauling on the part of the line that leads through a *movable* block, and " to least advantage" (or "disadvantage") when the hauling end first leads through a *fixed* block. Some of the more common purchases are shown in figure 43.

Strength of Fiber and Wire Rope

Fiber rope. Whenever the question arises as to how strong rope is or what weight it can withstand, the best means of finding out is to go to the manufacturer's specifications. If these specifications cannot be found, the empirical formula given below is useful and is surprisingly accurate. The formula is for Manila rope only, which is the standard. This gives an index for nylon, which is about two and a half times as strong as Manila of the same size. However, it is important to realize that rope that is not new, not stored properly, or is otherwise abused, is less strong than when it left the factory.

The following definitions and abbreviations are used with the formulas:

B = breaking strain (same as tensile strength), in terms of long tons or pounds as specified

C = circumference of rope

SWL or P = safe working load. Safety requires that less stress be placed on the rope or wire than is required to break it, otherwise the gear would frequently be carried away. If the SWL of Manila is used as 20 percent of B, and B of a 5-inch Manila is 20,250 pounds, then the SWL will be 4,050 pounds.

SF = safety factor—the relationship between B and the SWL. If the SWL of Manila as given in the above example is taken as 20 percent of B, the SF is 5.

Formulas:

$$B = \frac{C^2}{2.5} \qquad \text{or} \qquad B \times 900\ C^2$$

Where B is in long tons (2,240 pounds = 1 long ton) and C is in inches.	Where B is in pounds and C is in inches.

$$SWL = \frac{B}{SF}$$

In this formula, if SWL is in tons, B must be in tons. If SWL is in pounds, B must be in pounds.

Example: What is the breaking strain of 3-inch Manila in tons?

$$B = \frac{C^2}{2.5} = \frac{3^2}{2.5} = \frac{9}{2.5} = 3.6 \text{ long tons}$$

Example: What is the SWL if an SF of 6 is used?

$$SWL = \frac{B}{SF} = \frac{3.6}{6} = .6 \text{ long tons}$$

Formulas for wire rope. The formulas for wire rope are applied in the same manner as for fiber rope. They are

$$B = 2.5C^2 \text{ or } P \text{ or } SWL = \frac{C^2}{2.5}$$

Before applying the formulas you must remember the following:

Wire is measured by the diameter, not by the circumference, as is the case with fiber rope.

The formula assumes a safety factor of 6.25, which is generally used.

The formula holds good only for 6×12 plow steel or 6×24 cast steel wire. If any other wire is used, the factor of 2.5 will not work. Any seaman knows that the term 6×12 means that the wire rope has 6 strands, with 12 wires in each strand.

Marlinespike Seamanship

Marlinespike seamanship is a general term that covers all phases of rigging and rope work. It includes the care, han-

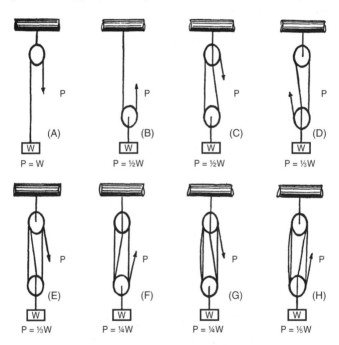

Fig. 43. Common purchases. "P" refers to the force of the pull, and "W" is the weight being lifted. In (A), 1 pound of pull lifts 1 pound of weight. In sketches (B) and (C), 1 pound of pull lifts 2 pounds of weight, and so on. (A) is a single whip and (B) is a single whip inverted or runner. (C) is a gun-tackle purchase rigged to least advantage, and (D) is the same purchase, but rigged to advantage. (E) is a luff tackle rigged to least advantage, and (F) is the same rigged to advantage. (A luff tackle is a combination of one single block and one double block.) (G) is a double or 2-fold purchase rigged to least advantage, and (H) is the same rigged to advantage.

dling, knotting, and splicing of both fiber and wire rope of all
sizes. A thorough knowledge of rigging and rope work is important to every seaman. The practical part of the able seaman examination may require knowledge about the knots,
splices, and canvas work illustrated in the following figures
(figs. 44–52).

Marlinespike seamanship hints. A splice or a knot
weakens a line. A spliced line retains 80 to 90% of its
strength, but a knot may reduce the strength by 50%.

Extra tucks should be put in splices of nylon or other synthetic ropes. Generally speaking, a splice in Manila, hemp,
or sisal should have three full tucks. Nylon or Dacron requires four full tucks and polypropylene should have a minimum of six.

An eye splice in wire rope used for cargo gear should be
given three full tucks with whole strands and two tucks with
one half the wire from the tucking strand.

Never pull on a kinked wire. You will ruin it. As soon as a
kink is noticed, grasp the part of each side of the wire outside
the kink and try to enlarge the kink by pushing and working
the wire into a loop. Turn the bent portion over, place on a
firm object, and push until the kink straightens out as much
as possible. Then, the area should be placed on a flat surface
and pounded smooth with a wooden mallet.

A shackle is stronger and safer than a hook of the same
size. If slings or rope may tend to jump out of the hook, mouse
the hook.

When a chain stopper is used to take the weight of a boom,
ease back the topping lift until the stopper has the weight before throwing off the turns from the warping head. Let the
stopper take the weight gradually.

If securing wire rope to cleats or bitts, always use a seizing of marline or other small stuff.

Use blocks large enough for the rope.

Most rope is right-handed and should be coiled clockwise.
Left-handed rope must be coiled counterclockwise or it will
kink.

Tarpaulins should be laid with the seams athwartships.
The top flap should be aft.

Fig. 44. Hitches: (A) two half hitches, (B) stage hitch, (C) timber hitch, (D) rolling hitch, (E) blackwall hitch, and (F) clove hitch.

Fig. 45. Knots: (A) overhand knot, (B) square knot, (C) figure eight knot, (D) wall knot, and (E) crown knot.

Fig. 46. Bends: (A) single sheet bend, (B) three strand Turk's head, (C) double sheet bend, (D) Carrick bend, and (E) fisherman's bend.

Fig. 47. (A) bowline, (B) bowline on a bight, (C) sheepshank, (D) French bowline, and (E) Spanish bowline.

Fig. 48. (A) monkey fist, (B) eye splice, and (C) eye splice in wire.

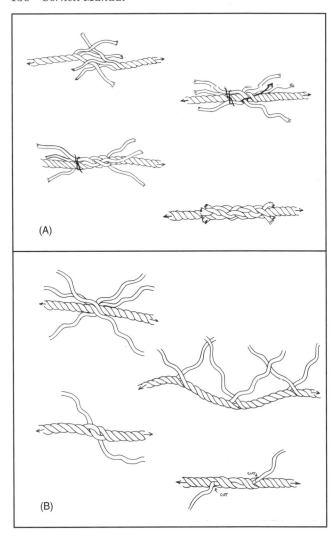

Fig. 49. (A) short splice, and (B) a long splice.

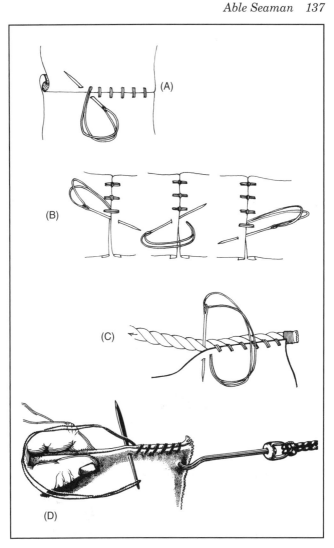

Fig. 50. Stitches: (A) flat stitch, (B) herringbone stitch, (C) sewing a bolt rope to canvas, and (D) round stitching canvas held by a bench hook.

Zinc should be used for a poured basket socket at the end of a wire rope. Babbitt metal or lead is not suitable.

U-bolts used on wire rope clips should fit over the short end of the wire (see figure 51).

Use seizings on the end of wire rope instead of welding. The heat from welding may weaken the wire. Whippings on the end of a fiber line keep it from unraveling (see figure 52).

Pollution

The continuous pollution of our inland and coastal waters has created new and stricter pollution control laws. The mariner must be aware of these laws and must know how to comply with them. He must have the professional skills to carry out his duties without being a hazard to the marine environment. In recent years the pollution laws have become more and more strict. Violations may result in a fine, loss of a license or merchant marine document, or both. The *Code of Federal Regulations* (33 CFR 151) contains detailed regulations for oil, transfer, and spill; garbage management and other pollution issues are covered by International Pollution Regulation (MARPOL).

Oil pollution causes serious damage and does it in many ways. It can destroy marine growth, kill birds, ruin beaches,

Fig. 51. Right and wrong way to use wire clips. Courtesy U.S. Navy.

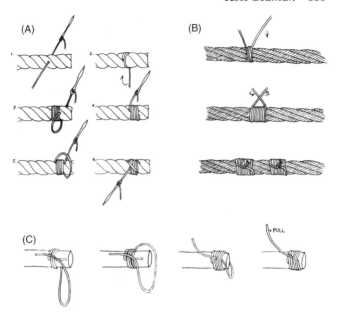

Fig. 52. (A) Palm and needle whipping on a line. (B) Putting temporary seizing on a wire rope. (C) Putting a temporary whipping on a line.

contaminate drinking supplies, and create fire hazards. The hazard of oil pollution is always present in normal operations such as deballasting, bilge cleaning, tank washing, refueling, and transfer operations. While most major spills are caused by large casualties such as collisions or groundings, most minor spills are caused by human error rather than equipment failure.

Pollution is a problem whether heavy or light oil is spilled, even though the slick from light oil tends to vaporize or dissolve. Vapor from light oil is poisonous to sea life even though it cannot be seen.

The law requires that the person in charge of a vessel notify the Coast Guard as soon as he knows of any oil discharge. Failure to do this can lead to a fine of $10,000, a year in jail, or both. Your company can be fined up to $5,000 for a spill, which is still less than the $10,000 charged for not reporting a spill.

The *Code of Federal Regulations (CFR)* states that only a licensed officer can be "the person in charge" of transfer operations on a tanker. On a tank barge this function may be performed by a certificated tankerman.

Space does not permit an adequate discussion of all regulations concerning pollution, transfer operations, and required procedures, but listing a few will give an idea of their scope:

1. Transfer operations cannot take place unless the vessel's moorings are strong enough to hold in all expected weather conditions and the hoses or arms are long enough to allow the vessel to move at its moorings without strain on the hose or arm.
2. Before a transfer operation, scuppers and drains must be plugged, flange couplings must be properly bolted, and an emergency shutdown system must be available.
3. Before the transfer, a meeting must be held between the person in charge on the vessel and the person in charge at the facility. Both persons in charge must agree to begin the transfer before it may be started.
4. Required lighting must be available for night transfer operations.
5. The Oil Pollution Act of 1990 prohibits the discharge of oil or oily mixtures within the prohibited zone. In general this is 50 miles offshore but may be extended to 100 miles.
6. A tank vessel must have a means of draining or removing discharge oil from each container or enclosed deck area without mixing incompatible products or discharging it into the water.
7. Oil transfer procedures must be printed in a language understood by the crew and permanently posted or available at the fueling or cargo control station.
8. No one may connect, top off, disconnect, or engage in any other critical oil transfer operation unless the person in charge is personally supervising these operations.

Fast Rescue Boat

A new requirement for rescue and safety on large vessels is that of carrying a fast rescue boat and certified personnel to operate and launch it (fig. 53). These rescue craft are stowed in special davits for easy and quick launching. The davit is equipped with a reserve power supply so that it can be operated without ship's power. The required competencies for certification in fast rescue boat operation are included with the other STCW requirements in appendix A.

Security

No text on seamanship would be complete without reference to special security training requirements and awareness. Ships have become potential targets of terrorist efforts, both in U.S. ports and around the world. Regulations now require that every vessel have a ship's security plan and a vessel security officer. The port facility and the ship-operating company also are required to appoint designated security officers. Special training is required of these security officers.

Fig. 53. A fast rescue boat in action.

In addition, every member of the crew is required to have a security assignment in the vessel security plan and training on security awareness. Model courses and regulations are currently being developed in each of these areas.

Sample Multiple-Choice Questions for the Able Seaman

The able seaman examination given by the Coast Guard consists of a written and a practical test as described in the *Code of Federal Regulations*. The written test is administered in two parts, each consisting of 50 multiple-choice questions in areas that include Rules of the Road, rigging, lifesaving and firefighting, pollution, and medical care. An overall grade of 70 percent in each part is required in order to pass. If the candidate is deficient in one area (Rules of the Road, for example), and he makes it up in other areas, he is still considered to have passed. He must, however, pass both parts in order to obtain the able seaman endorsement. The international code of signals (H.O. 102) and parts 155, 156, and 157 of Title 33 of the *Code of Federal Regulations* are available in the examining room. Lifeboat and liferaft questions that would duplicate the area covered in the sample questions for lifeboatmen are not included. Answers shown are those given in Coast Guard publications. The following questions are taken at random from published banks of Coast Guard Questions. The letter of the correct answer to each question is set in boldface type.

1. An example of a stock anchor is a(n) _____.
   a. articulated anchor
   b. Flipper Delta anchor
   c. hook anchor
   d. Danforth anchor

2. Which part of an anchor actually digs into the bottom?
   a. stock
   b. fluke
   c. shank
   d. crown

3. Buckler plates are _____.
   a. triangular-shaped plates connecting the bull chain to the topping lift
   b. metal plates secured over the tops of the hawse pipes
   c. faired shell plates with curvature in two directions
   d. sheets of dunnage used to prevent heavy cargo from buckling the deck plates

4. The safety stopper that prevents the anchor cable from running free if the cable jumps the wildcat is the _____.
   a. riding pawl
   b. devil's claw
   c. buckler plate
   d. spill pipe

5. The recessed areas on a wildcat are called _____.
   a. pawls
   b. sockets
   c. pockets
   d. whelps

6. How is the size of chain determined?
   a. length of link in inches
   b. diameter of metal in link in inches
   c. links per fathom
   d. weight of stud cable in pounds

7. How many turns of wire normally mark either side of the shackle 45 fathoms from the anchor?
   a. 1
   b. 2
   c. 3
   d. 4

8. Which of the following is NOT a duty of a lookout?
   a. Refuse to talk to others, except as required by duty.
   b. Remain standing during your watch

    c. Report every sighting
    d. Supervise any deck work going on in the area

9. A lookout should report objects sighted using _____.
    a. true bearings
    b. magnetic bearings
    c. gyro bearings
    d. relative bearings

10. While standing lookout duty at night, a dim light on the horizon will be seen quickest by looking: _____.
    a. at an area just a little below the horizon
    b. at the horizon, where the sky and the water appears to meet
    c. a little above the horizon
    d. well below the horizon line

11. You are standing wheelwatch on entering port, and the Master gives you a rudder command that conflicts with a rudder command from the Pilot. What should you do?
    a. Obey the Pilot.
    b. Obey the Master.
    c. Ask the Pilot for guidance.
    d. Bring the rudder to midships.

12. When relieving the helm, the new helmsman should know the _____.
    a. gyro error
    b. course per magnetic steering compass
    c. variation
    d. maximum rudder angle previously used

13. You are standing the wheelwatch when you hear the cry, "Man overboard starboard side." You should be ready to:
    a. give full right rudder
    b. give full left rudder
    c. put the rudder amidships
    d. throw a lifering to mark the spot

14. The helm command, "meet her" means _____.
    a. steer more carefully
    b. use the rudder to check the swing
    c. decrease the existing rudder angle
    d. note the course and steady on that bearing

15. When in pilotage waters, which type of steering should be in use?
    a. non-follow-up
    b. hand
    c. standby wheel
    d. automatic pilot

16. Your ship is steaming at night with the gyropilot engaged when you notice that the vessel's course is slowly changing to the right. Which of the following actions should you take FIRST?
    a. Notify the engine room of the steering malfunction.
    b. Change to telemotor (or other alternate steering system)
    c. Call the Master
    d. Send the quartermaster to the emergency steering station

17. You are on watch aboard a vessel heading NW with the wind from dead ahead, in heavy seas. You notice a man fall overboard from the starboard bow. Which of the following actions would NOT be appropriate?
    a. Hard right rudder
    b. Throw a life buoy to the man, if possible
    c. Send a man aloft
    d. Get the port boat ready

18. Which of the following is NOT an advantage of the Williamson turn?
    a. In a large vessel (VLCC) much of the headway will be lost thereby requiring little astern maneuvering.

b. When the turn is completed, the vessel will be on the original track line.

c. The initial actions are taken at well defined points and reduce the need for individual judgement.

d. The turn will return the vessel to the man's location in the shortest possible time.

19. A rescue helicopter hoist area would preferably have a minimum radius of at least _____.
   a. 6 feet of clear deck
   b. 10 feet of clear deck
   c. 25 feet of clear deck
   d. 50 feet of clear deck

20. When anchoring a vessel under normal conditions, what scope of chain is recommended?
   a. four times the depth of water
   b. two and one-half times the depth of water
   c. five to seven times the depth of water
   d. fifteen times the depth of water.

21. The strongest of the natural fibers is _____.
   a. cotton
   b. hemp
   c. Manila
   d. sisal

22. Line is called "small stuff" if its circumference is less than _____.
   a. $\frac{1}{2}''$
   b. $\frac{3}{4}''$
   c. $1''$
   d. $1\frac{3}{4}''$

23. As you hold a piece of Manila line vertically in front of you, the strands run from the lower left to the upper right. What type of line is this?
   a. right-hand laid

b. cable-laid

c. sennet-laid

d. water-laid

24. In order to clean a mooring line that is full of mud and sand, the line should be _____.

    a. hosed down with fresh water

    b. hosed down with salt water

    c. scrubbed with detergent and water

    d. steam cleaned with high pressure steam

25. Which of the following types of line would BEST be able to withstand sudden shock loads?

    a. polypropylene

    b. nylon

    c. Dacron

    d. Manila

26. The critical point in nylon line elongation is considered to be:

    a. 20%

    b. 30%

    c. 40%

    d. 50%

27. A mooring line is described as being 6 × 24, 1¾ inch wire rope. What do the above numbers refer to?

    a. strands, yarns, circumference

    b. strands, wires, diameter

    c. wires, yarns, diameter

    d. strands, circumference, wires

28. A rope made of a combination of wire and fiber is known as _____.

    a. independent

    b. lang lay

    c. preformed

    d. spring lay

29. Galvanizing would NOT be suitable for protecting a wire rope which is used for _____.
   a. cargo runners
   b. mooring wires
   c. shrouds
   d. stays

30. The ultimate or maximum strength of a wire rope is referred to as the _____.
   a. operating strength
   b. working load
   c. breaking strength
   d. lifting load

31. If kinking results while wire rope is being coiled clockwise, you should _____.
   a. coil it counter clockwise
   b. not coil it
   c. take a turn under
   d. twist out the kinks under a strain

32. Mousing a cargo hook with marline or small line _____.
   a. increases the lifting capacity of the hook
   b. protects the hook from the sling ring
   c. prevents the sling ring from coming out of the hook
   d. all of the above

33. When rigging a bosun's chair on a stay with a shackle, _____.
   a. mouse the shackle to the chair
   b. never allow the shackle pin to ride on the stay
   c. secure it with small stuff
   d. seize the end of the shackle

34. A mooring line that checks forward motion of a vessel at a pier is a _____.
   a. bow line
   b. forward bow line

   c. stern line
   d. stern breast line

35. Which mooring line is likely to undergo the most strain when docking a ship under normal conditions?
   a. bow line
   b. breast line
   c. spring line
   d. stern line

36. To "belay" a line means _____.
   a. coil it down
   b. heave it taut
   c. stow it below
   d. secure it to a cleat

37. You are handling a mooring line and you are instructed to "Check the line." What should be done?
   a. You should ensure the bight is not fouled between the ship and dock by taking up the slack.
   b. The line is paid out smartly and kept free for running.
   c. The line should be secured by adding more turns and then the area should be cleared.
   d. The line is surged so that it maintains a strain without parting.

38. When a line is laid down in loose, looping figure eights, it is said to be _____.
   a. faked
   b. flemished
   c. coiled
   d. chined

39. A "figure-eight" knot is used to _____.
   a. be a stopper
   b. shorten a line
   c. join lines of equal size
   d. keep a line from passing through a sheave

40. What knot or bend is used to tie a small line to a larger one?
    a. becket bend
    b. bowline
    c. clove hitch
    d. lark's head

41. The knot used to join two lines or two large hawsers for towing is called a _____.
    a. square knot
    b. carrick bend
    c. sheet bend
    d. bowline

42. You need to make a fixed loop at the end of a line in order to use the line as a mooring line. You have no time to make a splice. Which knot should you use?
    a. bowline
    b. figure-eight
    c. overhand
    d. round-turn and two half hitches

43. A "whipping" is _____.
    a. a messenger
    b. a stopper for nylon line
    c. a U-bolt for securing a cargo whip to the winch drum
    d. twine tied around a rope end

44. A splice that can be used in running rigging, where the line will pass through blocks, is a _____.
    a. short splice
    b. long splice
    c. back splice
    d. spindle splice

45. The correct way to make an eye in a wire rope with clips is to place the clips with the _____.
    a. first and third U-bolts on the bitter end and the second U-bolt on the standing part

b. first and third U-bolts on the standing part and the second U-bolt on the bitter end

c. U-bolts of all clips on the bitter end

d. U-bolts of all clips on the standing part

46. What is the name of this tackle?
    a. whip
    b. one fold purchase
    c. gun tackle
    d. runner

47. A snatch block would most likely be used as a _____.
    a. boat fall
    b. fairlead
    c. riding pawl
    d. topping lift

48. What size block shell should be used with a 4-inch Manila line?
    a. 8″
    b. 12″
    c. 16″
    d. 24″

49. Unless extremely flexible wire rope is used, the sheave diameter should always be as large as possible, but should NEVER be less than _____.
    a. 20 times the rope diameter
    b. 10 times the rope diameter
    c. 2 times the rope diameter
    d. the rope diameter

50. When a block and tackle is "rove to advantage," this means that the _____.
    a. blocks have been overhauled
    b. hauling parts of two tackles are attached
    c. hauling part leads through the movable block
    d. hauling part leads through the standing block

51. Most minor spills of oil products are caused by _____.
    a. equipment failure
    b. human error
    c. major casualties
    d. unforeseeable circumstances

52. Heavy fuel oils when spilled are _____.
    a. more harmful to sea life than lighter oils
    b. easier to clean up than lighter refined oils
    c. less harmful to sea life than lighter oils
    d. not a real threat to marine life

53. Which statement is TRUE of a gasoline spill?
    a. It is visible for a shorter time than a fuel oil spill.
    b. It is not covered by pollution laws.
    c. It does little harm to marine life.
    d. It will sink more rapidly than crude oil.

54. In reference to accidental oil pollution, the most critical time during bunkering is when _____.
    a. you first start to receive fuel
    b. hoses are being blown down
    c. final topping off is occurring
    d. hoses are being disconnected

55. Except in rare cases, it is impossible to extinguish a shipboard fire by _____.
    a. removing the heat
    b. removing the oxygen
    c. removing the fuel
    d. interrupting the chain reaction

56. What is required in addition to the heat, fuel, and oxygen of the fire triangle to have a fire?
    a. smoke
    b. electricity
    c. pressure
    d. chain reaction

57. The spread of fire is prevented by _____.
   a. cooling surfaces adjacent to the fire
   b. removing combustibles from the endangered area
   c. shutting off the oxygen supply
   d. all of the above

58. What, when removed, will result in the extinguishment of a fire?
   a. nitrogen
   b. sodium
   c. oxygen
   d. carbon dioxide

59. All of the following are part of the fire triangle except

   _____.
   a. heat
   b. oxygen
   c. electricity
   d. fuel

60. If ignited, which material would be a class B fire?
   a. magnesium
   b. paper
   c. wood
   d. diesel oil

61. A triangular daymark would be colored _____.
   a. red
   b. red and white
   c. green
   d. green and white

62. Deviation is caused by _____.
   a. changes in the earth's magnetic field
   b. nearby magnetic land masses or mineral deposits
   c. magnetic influence inherent to that particular vessel
   d. all of the above

63. What is the mark on a lead line indicating 10 fathoms?
    a. one knot
    b. one strip of leather
    c. leather with a hole
    d. no marking

64. The four standard light colors used for lighted aids to navigation are red, green, white and _____.
    a. purple
    b. orange
    c. blue
    d. yellow

65. The magnetic compass error which changes with the geographical location of your vessel is called _____.
    a. deviation
    b. variation
    c. compensation
    d. differentiation

66. First aid means _____.
    a. medical treatment of accident
    b. setting of broken bones
    c. emergency treatment at the scene of the injury
    d. dosage of medications

67. When giving first aid, you should understand how to conduct primary and secondary surveys and know _____.
    a. which medications to prescribe
    b. how to diagnose an illness from symptoms
    c. the limits of your capabilities
    d. how to set broken bones

68. In managing a situation involving multiple injuries, the rescuer must be able to _____.
    a. provide the necessary medication
    b. rapidly evaluate the seriousness of obvious injuries
    c. accurately diagnose the ailment or injury
    d. prescribe treatment for the victim

69. A compound fracture is a fracture _____.
    a. in which more than one bone is broken
    b. in which the same bone is broken in more than one place
    c. which is never accompanied by internal bleeding
    d. in which the bone may be visible

70. BOTH INTERNATIONAL & INLAND. If you saw flames aboard a vessel but could see the vessel was not on fire, you would know that _____.
    a. the crew was trying to get warm
    b. the vessel required immediate assistance
    c. the vessel was attempting to attract the attention of a pilot boat
    d. the vessel was being illuminated for identification by aircraft

71. BOTH INTERNATIONAL & INLAND. Five or more short blasts on a vessel's whistle indicates that she is _____.
    a. in doubt that another vessel is taking sufficient action to avoid collision
    b. altering course to starboard
    c. altering course to port
    d. the stand-on vessel and will maintain course and speed

72. BOTH INTERNATIONAL & INLAND. You are watching another vessel and its compass bearing does not change. This would indicate that _____.
    a. you are the stand-on vessel
    b. a risk of collision exists
    c. a special circumstances situation exists
    d. the other vessel is dead in the water

73. BOTH INTERNATIONAL & INLAND. While underway and making way your vessel enters fog. What fog signal should you sound every two minutes?
    a. one prolonged blast
    b. two prolonged blasts

c. three short blasts
d. a prolonged blast and two short blasts

74. BOTH INTERNATIONAL & INLAND. When two power-driven vessels are meeting head-on and there is a risk of collision, each shall _____.
a. stop her engines
b. alter course to starboard
c. sound the danger signal
d. back down

75. A true bearing of a charted object, when plotted on a chart, will establish a _____.
a. fix
b. line of position
c. relative bearing
d. range

5. Qualified Member
of the Engine Department (QMED)

The following information concerning requirements and certification as a qualified member of the engine department is reproduced from the *Code of Federal Regulations: Title 46—Shipping,* Subparts 12.15 (Washington, D.C.: U.S. Government Printing Office, 1999). STCW certification is also required for QMEDs. As with able seamen, the STCW competencies from the IMO Code are included in appendix A of this manual. The international term for QMED is "ratings forming part of the engineering watch."

Subpart 12.15—Qualified Member of the Engine Department

Sec. 12.15-1 Certification required.

(a) Every person employed in a rating as qualified member of the engine department on any United States vessel requiring certificated qualified members of the engine department shall produce a certificate as qualified member of the engine department to the shipping commissioner, United States Collector or Deputy Collector of Customs, or master before signing articles of agreement.

(b) No certificate as qualified member of the engine department is required of any person employed on any un-rigged vessel, except seagoing barges.

Sec. 12.15-3 General requirements.

(a) A qualified member of the engine department is any person below the rating of licensed officer and above the rating of coal passer or wiper, who holds a certificate of service as such qualified member of the engine department issued by the Coast Guard or predecessor authority.

(b) For purposes of administering this part the rating of *assistant electrician* is considered a rating not above that of coal passer or wiper, but equal thereto.

(c) An applicant, to be eligible for certification as qualified member of the engine department, shall be able to speak and understand the English language as would be required in the rating of qualified member of the engine department and in an emergency aboard ship.

(d) After July 31, 1998, an STCW endorsement valid for any period on or after February 1, 2002, will be issued or renewed only when the candidate for certification as a qualified member of the engine department also produces satisfactory evidence, on the basis of assessment of a practical demonstration of skills and abilities, of having achieved or maintained within the previous 5 years the minimum standards of competence for the following 4 areas of basic safety:

(1) Personal survival techniques as set out in table A-VI/1-1 of the STCW Code (incorporated by reference in Sec. 12.01-3).

(2) Fire prevention and fire-fighting as set out in table A-VI/1-2 of the STCW Code.

(3) Elementary first aid as set out in table A-VI/1-3 of the STCW Code.

(4) Personal safety and social responsibilities as set out in table A-VI/1-4 of the STCW Code.

(e) After July 31, 1998 an STCW endorsement that is valid for any period on or after February 1, 2002, will be issued or renewed only when the candidate for certification as a qualified member of the engine department meets the standards of competence set out in STCW Regulation III/4 and Section A-III/4 of the STCW Code, if the candidate will be serving as a rating forming part of a watch in a manned engine-room, or designated to perform duties in a periodically unmanned engine-room, on a seagoing ship driven by main propulsion machinery of 750 kW [1,000 hp] propulsion power or more.

[CGFR 65-50, 30 FR 16640, Dec. 30, 1965, as amended by CGD 95-062, 62 FR 34538, June 26, 1997; USCG-2000-7790, 65 FR 58458, Sept. 29, 2000; USCG- 1999-5610, 67 FR 66069, Oct. 30, 2002]

Sec. 12.15-5 Physical requirements.

(a) An applicant for a certificate of service as a qualified member of the engine department shall present a certificate of a medical officer of the United States Public Health Service, or other reputable physician attesting that his eyesight, hearing, and physical condition are such that he can perform the duties required of a qualified member of the engine department.

(b) The medical examination for qualified member of the engine department is the same as for an original license as engineer, as set forth in Sec. 10.205 of this subchapter. If the applicant is in possession of an unexpired license, the Officer in Charge, Marine Inspection, may waive the requirement for a physical examination.

(c) An applicant holding a certificate of service for a particular rating as qualified member of the engine department and desiring certification for another rating covered by this same form of certificate may qualify therefor without a physical examination unless the Officer in Charge, Marine Inspection, finds that the applicant obviously suffers from some physical or mental infirmity to a degree that would render him incompetent to perform the ordinary duties of a qualified member of the engine department. In this event the applicant shall be required to undergo an examination to determine his competency.

[CGFR 65-50, 30 FR 16640, Dec. 30, 1965, as amended by USCG-1998-4442, 63 FR 52189, Sept. 30, 1998]

Sec. 12.15-7 Service or training requirements.

(a) An applicant for a certificate of service as qualified member of the engine department shall furnish the Coast Guard proof of qualification based on six months' service in a rating at least equal to that of wiper or coal passer.

(b) Training programs approved by the Commanding Officer, National Maritime Center, may be substituted for the required service at sea in accordance with the following:

(1) A graduate of a school ship may be rated as qualified member of the engine department upon satisfactory completion of the course of instruction. For this purpose, *school ship*

is interpreted to mean an institution which offers a complete course of instruction, including a period of sea training, in the skills appropriate to the rating of qualified member of the engine department.

(2) Training programs other than those classified as a school ship may be substituted for up to one-half of the required service at sea.

(c) To qualify to receive an STCW endorsement for service as a "rating forming part of a watch in a manned engine-room or designated to perform duties in a periodically unmanned engine-room" on a seagoing vessel driven by main propulsion machinery 750 kW [1,000 hp] propulsion power or more, an applicant shall prove seagoing service that includes training and experience associated with engine-room watchkeeping and involves the performance of duties carried out under the direct supervision of a qualified engineer officer or a member of a qualified rating. The training must establish that the applicant has achieved the standard of competence prescribed in table A-III/4 of the STCW Code (incorporated by reference in Sec. 12.01-3), in accordance with the methods of demonstrating competence and the criteria for evaluating competence specified in that table. [CGD 80-131, 45 FR 69241, Oct. 20, 1980, as amended by CGD 95-072, 60 FR 50460, Sept. 29, 1995; CGD 95-062, 62 FR 34538, June 26, 1997; CGD 95-062, 62 FR 40140, July 25, 1997; USCG-1998-4442, 63 FR 52189, Sept. 30, 1998; USCG-1999-5610, 67 FR 66069, Oct. 30, 2002]

Sec. 12.15-9 Examination requirements.

(a) Each applicant for certification as a qualified member of the engine department in the rating of oiler, watertender, fireman, deck engineer, refrigeration engineer, junior engineer, electrician, or machinist shall be examined orally or by other means and only in the English language on the subjects listed in paragraph (b) of this section. The applicant's general knowledge of the subjects must be sufficient to satisfy the examiner that he is qualified to perform the duties of the rating for which he makes application.

(b) List of subjects required:

Subject	Machinist	Refrigerating engineer	Fireman/Watertender	Oiler	Electrician	Junior engineer	Deck engineer
1. Application, maintenance, and use of hand tools and measuring instruments	x	x	x	x	x	x	x
2. Uses of babbitt, copper, brass, steel, and other metals	x	x	x	x	x	x	x
3. Methods of measuring pipe, pipe fittings, sheet metal, machine bolts and nuts, packing, etc.	x	x	x	x	x	x	x
4. Operation and maintenance of mechanical remote control equipment	x		x	x	x	x	x
5. Precautions to be taken for the prevention of fire and the proper use of firefighting equipment	x	x	x	x	x	x	x
6. Principles of mechanical refrigeration; and functions, operation, and maintenance of various machines and parts of the systems		x		x		x	
7. Knowledge of piping systems as used in ammonia, freon, and CO_2, including testing for leaks, operation of bypasses, and making up of joints		x				x	
8. Safety precautions to be observed in the operation of various refrigerating systems, including storage of refrigerants, and the use of gas masks and firefighting equipment	x	x	x	x	x	x	x
9. Combustion of fuels, proper temperature, pressures, and atomization			x	x		x	
10. Operation of the fuel oil system on oil burning boilers, including the transfer and storage of fuel oil			x	x		x	x
11. Hazards involved and the precautions taken against accumulation of oil in furnaces, bilges, floorplates, and tank tops; flarebacks, leaks in fuel oil heaters, clogged strainers and burner tips	x	x	x	x	x	x	x

Subject	Machinist	Refrigerating engineer	Fireman/Watertender	Oiler	Electrician	Junicr engineer	Deck engineer
12. Precautions necessary when filling empty boilers, starting up the fuel oil burning system, and raising steam from a cold boiler			x	x		x	
13. The function, operation, and maintenance of the various engineroom auxiliaries	x	x	x	x	x	x	
14. Proper operation of the various types of lubricating systems	x	x	x	x	x	x	x
15. Safety precautions to be observed in connection with the operation of engineroom auxiliaries, electrical machinery, and switchboard equipment	x	x	x	x	x	x	x
16. The function, operation, and maintenance of the bilge, ballast, fire, freshwater, sanitary, and lubricating systems	x	x	x	x		x	x
17. Proper care of spare machine parts and idle equipment	x	x	x	x	x	x	x
18. The procedure in preparing a turbine, reciprocating, or Diesel engine for standby; also the procedure in securing			x	x		x	
19. Operation and maintenance of the equipment necessary for the supply of water to boilers, the dangers of high and low water and remedial action			x	x		x	
20. Operation, location, and maintenance of the various boiler fittings and accessories	x		x	x		x	
21. The practical application and solution of basic electrical calculations (Ohm's law, power formula, etc.)					x	x	x
22. Electrical wiring circuits of the various two-wire and three-wire D.C. systems and the various single-phase and polyphase A.C. systems					x	x	x
23. Application and characteristics of parallel and series circuits					x	x	x

Subject	Machinist	Refrigerating engineer	Fireman/Watertender	Oiler	Electrician	Junior engineer	Deck engineer
24. Application and maintenance of electrical meters and instruments					x	x	x
25. The maintenance and installation of lighting and power wiring involving testing for, locating, and correcting grounds, short circuits and open circuits, and making splices					x	x	x
26. The operation and maintenance of the various types of generators and motors, both A.C. and D.C.					x	x	x
27. Operation, installation, and maintenance of the various types of electrical controls and safety devices					x	x	x
28. Testing and maintenance of special electrical equipment, such as telegraphs, telephones, alarm systems, fire-detecting systems, and rudder angle indicators					x	x	
29. Rules and Regulations and requirements for installation, repair, and maintenance of electrical wiring and equipment installed aboard ships.					x	x	x
29a. Pollution laws and regulations, procedures for discharge containment and cleanup, and methods for disposal of sludge and waste from cargo and fueling operations	x	x	x	x	x	x	
30. Such further examination of a nonmathematical character as the Officer in Charge, Marine Inspection, may consider necessary to establish the applicant's proficiency	x	x	x	x	x	x	x

(c) Each applicant for certification as a qualified member of the engine department in the rating of pumpman shall, by oral or other examination, demonstrate sufficient knowledge of the subjects peculiar to that rating to satisfy the Officer in Charge, Marine Inspection, that he or she is qualified to perform the duties of that rating.

(d) Applicants for certification as qualified members of the engine department in the rating of deck engine mechanic or engineman, who have proved eligibility for such endorsement under either Sec. 12.15-13 or Sec. 12.15-15, will not be required to take a written or oral examination for such ratings.

[CGFR 65-50, 30 FR 16640, Dec. 30, 1965, as amended by CGFR 66-46, 31 FR 13649, Oct. 22, 1966; CGD 71-161R, 37 FR 28263, Dec. 21, 1972; CGD 74- 75, 42 FR 24741, May 16, 1977; CGD 94-029, 61 FR 47064, Sept. 6, 1996]

Sec. 12.15-11 General provisions respecting merchant mariner's documents endorsed as qualified member of the engine department.

The holder of a merchant mariner's document endorsed with one or more qualified member of the engine department ratings may serve in any unqualified rating in the engine department without obtaining an additional endorsement. This does not mean that an endorsement of one qualified member of the engine department rating authorizes the holder to serve in all qualified member of the engine department ratings. Each qualified member of the engine department rating for which a holder of a merchant mariner's document is qualified must be endorsed separately. When, however, the applicant qualifies for all ratings covered by a certificate as a qualified member of the engine department, the certification may read *QMED—any rating*. The ratings are as follows:

(a) Refrigerating engineer.

(b) Oiler.

(c) Deck engineer.

(d) Fireman/Watertender.

(e) Junior engineer.

(f) Electrician.

(g) Machinist.

(h) Pumpman.

(i) Deck engine mechanic.

(j) Engineman.
[CGFR 65-50, 30 FR 16640, Dec. 30, 1965, as amended by CGFR 66-46, 31 FR 13649, Oct. 22, 1966; CGD 74-45, 42 FR 24741, May 16, 1977]

Sec. 12.15-13 Deck engine mechanic.

(a) An applicant for a certificate as *deck engine mechanic* shall be a person holding a merchant mariner's document endorsed as *junior engineer.* The applicant shall be eligible for such certification upon furnishing one of the following:

(1) Satisfactory documentary evidence of sea service of 6 months in the rating of *junior engineer* on steam vessels of 4,000 horsepower or over; or,

(2) Documentary evidence from an operator of an automated vessel that he has completed satisfactorily at least 4 weeks indoctrination and training in the engine department of an automated steam vessel of 4,000 horsepower or over; or,

(3) Satisfactory completion of a course of training for *deck engine mechanic* acceptable to the Commanding Officer, National Maritime Center.

(b) The Officer in Charge, Marine Inspection, who is satisfied that an applicant for the rating of *deck engine mechanic* meets the requirements specified in this section, will endorse this rating on the current merchant mariner's document held by the applicant.

(c) Any holder of a merchant mariner's document endorsed *for any unlicensed rating in the engine department or QMED—any rating is qualified as a deck engine mechanic* and that endorsement will not be entered on his document. [CGFR 66-46, 31 FR 13649, Oct. 22, 1966, as amended by CGD 95-072, 60 FR 50460, Sept. 29, 1995; CGD 95-028, 62 FR 51196, Sept. 30, 1997; USCG- 1998-4442, 63 FR 52189, Sept. 30, 1998]

Sec. 12.15-15 Engineman.

(a) An applicant for a certificate as *engineman* shall be a person holding a merchant mariner's document endorsed as *fireman/watertender* and *oiler,* or *junior engineer.* The applicant shall be eligible for such certification upon furnishing one of the following:

(1) Satisfactory documentary evidence of sea service of 6 months in any one or combination of *junior engineer, fireman/watertender* or *oiler* on steam vessels of 4,000 horsepower or over; or,

(2) Documentary evidence from an operator of a *partially automated* steam vessel that he has completed satisfactorily at least 2 weeks indoctrination and training in the engine department of a *partially automated* steam vessel of 4,000 horsepower or over; or

(3) Satisfactory completion of a course of training for *engineman* acceptable to the Commanding Officer, National Maritime Center.

(b) The Officer in Charge, Marine Inspection, who is satisfied that an applicant for the rating of *engineman* meets the requirements specified in this section, will endorse this rating on the current merchant mariner's document held by the applicant.

(c) Any holder of a merchant mariner's document endorsed for *any unlicensed rating in the engine department, QMED—any rating or deck engine mechanic* is qualified as an *engineman* and that endorsement will not be entered on his document.

[CGFR 66-46, 31 FR 13650, Oct. 22, 1966, as amended by CGD 95-072, 60 FR 50460, Sept. 29, 1995; CGD 95-028, 62 FR 51196, Sept. 30, 1997; USCG-1998-4442, 63 FR 52189, Sept. 30, 1998]

Appendix A: STCW—Code Extracts

Table A-II/4
Specification of minimum standard of competence for ratings forming part of a navigational watch

Knowledge, understanding, and proficiency:

Use of magnetic and gyro-compasses

Helm orders

Change-over from automatic pilot to hand steering and vice versa

Responsibilities of a look-out, including reporting the approximate bearing of a sound signal, light or other object in degrees or points

Shipboard terms and definitions

Use of appropriate internal communication and alarm systems

Ability to understand orders and to communicate with the officer of the watch in matters relevant to watch-keeping duties

Procedures for the relief, maintenance and handover of a watch

Information required to maintain a safe watch

Basic environmental protection procedures

Knowledge of emergency duties and alarm signals

Knowledge of pyrotechnic distress signals; satellite EPIRBs and SARTs

Avoidance of false distress alerts and action to be taken in event of accidental activation

Table A-III/4
Specification of minimum standard of competence for ratings forming part of an engineering watch

Knowledge, understanding, and proficiency:

Terms used in machinery spaces and names of machinery and equipment

Engine-room watchkeeping procedures

Safe working practices as related to engine-room operations

Basic environmental protection procedures

Use of appropriate internal communication system

Engine-room alarm systems and ability to distinguish between the various alarms, with special reference to fire-extinguishing gas alarms

Safe operation of boilers

Knowledge of emergency duties

Escape routes from machinery spaces

Familiarity with the location and use of firefighting equipment in the machinery spaces

Table A-VI/I-I
Specification of minimum standard of competence in personal survival techniques

Knowledge, understanding, and proficiency:

Types of emergency situations that may occur, such as collision, fire, foundering

Types of life-saving appliances normally carried on ships

Equipment in survival craft

Location of personal life-saving appliances

Principles concerning survival, including:

1. value of training and drills
2. personal protective clothing and equipment
3. need to be ready for any emergency
4. actions to be taken when called to survival craft stations
5. actions to be taken when required to abandon ship
6. actions to be taken when in the water

Table A-VI/1-4
Specification of minimum standard of competence in personal safety and social responsibilities

Knowledge, understanding, and proficiency:

Types of emergency which may occur, such as collision, fire, foundering

Knowledge of shipboard contingency plans for response to emergencies

Emergency signals and specific duties allocated to crew members in the muster list; muster stations; correct use of personal safety equipment

Action to take on discovering potential emergency, including fire, collision, foundering, and ingress of water into the ship

Action to take on hearing emergency alarm signals

Value of training and drills

Knowledge of escape routes and internal communication and alarm systems

Effects of operational or accidental pollution of the marine environment

Basic environmental protection procedures

Table A-VI/1-2
Specification of minimum standard of competence in fire prevention and fire fighting

Knowledge, understanding and proficiency:

Shipboard fire-fighting organization

Location of fire-fighting appliances and emergency escape routes

The elements of fire and explosion (the fire triangle)

Types and sources of ignition

Flammable materials, fire hazards and spread of fire

The need for constant vigilance

Actions to be taken on board ship

Fire and smoke detection and automatic alarm systems

Classification of fire and applicable extinguishing agents

Appendix B:
United States Coast Guard
Regional Examination Centers
(RECs)

Examinations for the ratings for which this book has been prepared are given at each of the Coast Guard Regional Examination Centers (RECs) listed below. RECs are prepared not only to administer examinations, but also to provide information about procedures and about Coast Guard services available at other facilities.

It is suggested that candidates write or phone their nearest REC for specific information.

Alaska

U.S. Coast Guard, Marine Safety Office (REC)
800 E. Diamond Blvd., Suite 3-227
Anchorage, AK 99515
(907) 271-6736

U.S. Coast Guard, Marine Safety Office (REC)
2760 Sherwood Lane, Suite 2A
Juneau, AK 99801-8545
(907) 463-2458

California

U.S. Coast Guard, Marine Safety Office (REC)
1001 S. Seaside Avenue, Bldg. 20
San Pedro, CA 90731-0208
(310) 732-2080

U.S. Coast Guard, Marine Safety Office (REC)
Oakland Federal Building, North Tower
1301 Clay Street, Room 180N
Oakland, CA 94612-5200
(510) 637-1124

Florida

U.S. Coast Guard, Marine Safety Office (REC)
Claude Pepper Federal Bldg., 6th Floor
51 S.W. First Avenue
Miami, FL 33130-1608
(305) 536-6548/6874

Hawaii

U.S. Coast Guard, Marine Safety Office (REC)
433 Ala Moana Boulevard
Honolulu, HI 96813-4909
(808) 522-8264

Louisiana

U.S. Coast Guard, Marine Safety Office (REC)
9820 Lake Forest Blvd., Suite P
New Orleans, LA 70127-3077
(504) 240-7300

Maryland

U.S. Coast Guard, Marine Safety Office (REC)
U.S. Custom House
40 S. Gay Street
Baltimore, MD 21202-4022
(410) 962-5132

Massachusetts

U.S. Coast Guard, Marine Safety Office (REC)
455 Commercial Street
Boston, MA 02109-1045
(617) 223-3040

Missouri

U.S. Coast Guard, Marine Safety Office (REC)
1222 Spruce Street, Suite 8.104E
St. Louis, MO 63103-2835
(314) 539-3091

New York

U.S. Coast Guard, Marine Inspection Office (REC)
Battery Park Building
1 South Street
New York, NY 10004-1466
(212) 668-7492

Ohio

U.S. Coast Guard, Marine Safety Office (REC)
420 Madison Avenue, Suite 700
Toledo, OH 43604
(419) 418-6010

Oregon

U.S. Coast Guard, Marine Safety Office (REC)
6767 N. Basin Avenue
Portland, OR 97217-3992
(503) 240-9346

South Carolina

U.S. Coast Guard, Marine Safety Office (REC)
196 Tradd Street
Charleston, SC 29401-1899
(843) 720-3250

Tennessee

U.S. Coast Guard, Marine Safety Office (REC)
200 Jefferson Avenue, Suite 1302
Memphis, TN 38103
(901) 544-3297

Texas

U.S. Coast Guard, Marine Safety Office (REC)
8876 Gulf Freeway, Suite 200
Houston, TX 77017-6595
(713) 948-3350/51

Washington

U.S. Coast Guard, Marine Safety Office (REC)
915 Second Ave., Room 194
Seattle, WA 98174-1067
(206) 217-6115

References

The following publications are suggested for further study:

Bowditch, Nathaniel (original author). *American Practical Navigator* (Pub. No. 9). Washington, D.C.: United States Government Printing Office, 1995.

Hayler, William B., John M. Keever, and Paul M. Seiler, eds. *American Merchant Seaman's Manual.* 7th ed. Centreville, Md.: Cornell Maritime Press, 2003.

Huber, Mark. *Tanker Operations: A Handbook for the Person-in-Charge (PIC),* 4th ed. Centreville, Md.: Cornell Maritime Press, 2001.

International Code of Signals. (Pub. No. 102). Bethesda, Md.: National Imagery and Mapping Agency, 2003.

Krabbenschmidt, Dale. *Marine Firefighting Training Manual.* Oakland, Calif.: Military Sealift Command, Pacific, 1980.

Maloney, Elbert S., ed. *Dutton's Navigation and Piloting.* 14th ed. Annapolis, Md.: Naval Institute Press, 1985.

A Manual for the Safe Handling of Flammable and Combustible Liquids and Other Hazardous Products (CG-174). Washington, D.C.: Department of Transportation, U.S. Coast Guard, 1976.

Marine Fire Prevention, Firefighting, and Fire Safety. Washington, D.C.: Department of Commerce, Maritime Administration, 1988.

Navigation Rules, International-Inland. Washington, D.C.: Department of Transportation, U.S. Coast Guard, 1999.

Meurn, Robert J., and Charles L. Sauerbier. *Marine Cargo Operations.* 3d ed. Centreville, Md.: Cornell Maritime Press, 2004.

Shipboard Guide for Pollution-Free Operations. Washington, D.C.: Maritime Administration, 1976.

U.S. Public Health Service. *The Ship's Medicine Chest and Medical Aid at Sea.* La Vergne, Tenn.: Lightning Source, Inc., 2001.

About the Authors

John Keever is a graduate of the California Maritime Academy and has his M.A. from Golden Gate University. He is a commander in the Merchant Marine Reserve of the U.S. Navy and Master of the T.S. *Golden Bear*.

The late William B. Hayler was a graduate of the U.S. Naval Academy and received his M.A. from George Washington University. During World War II he served aboard the USS *Franklin* (CV-13) when she suffered near-fatal damage off Japan but returned to New York under her own power. Subsequently he commanded the LST 859, the LSMR 403 during the Korean War, the high-speed transport *Balduck*, the destroyer *Buck*, and the repair ship *Cadmus*.

The late Paul Seiler retired from the Coast Guard as a Chief Warrant Boatswain and served aboard the attack transport *Hunter Liggett* and *Etamin*, a liberty ship, during World War II. Before joining the California Maritime Academy he spent eight years at the Coast Guard Academy as Chief Boatswain of the *Eagle*, the 295-foot barque, which makes the annual training cruises for Coast Guard midshipmen.

ISBN 0-87033-559-6